Prai___ ___
The Heart of an Artichoke

"As though guided by the Horatian precept for poetry, this enthusiastic book delights and teaches simultaneously. If you are an *amateur* of French who wants either to expand your familiarity or to improve your proficiency, this is your *livre de chevet* — unless you fear being kept awake. A book for students who prefer to find the language embedded in the culture, it is also for venturesome teachers, because it proves the benefits of combining piecemeal appropriation with task-based absorption. The innovative *mise en page* stitches together dialogue, anecdote, quotation, and vivacious vignette in an invigorating and inspiring collage."

> — *Stephen Yenser, Distinguished Research Professor at UCLA, author of* The Fire in All Things, *winner of the Walt Whitman Award*

"Claire Lerognon and Linda Phillips Ashour's passionate involvement with and conversation about *la langue française* help debunk stereotypes about speaking, reading, and writing in a second language. Being responsible for the organization's language and communication training efforts, I commend their work in *The Heart of an Artichoke* as an homage to learning and a tool for cultural understanding."

> — *Atul Khare, United Nations Under-Secretary-General for Operational Support*

"Over several lonely months during the fall–winter of 1968–69, I practiced my French while wandering the streets of Paris, reading signs, advertisements, restaurant menus, historical markers out loud to myself. I was too depressed to realize that I was teaching myself about the intricacies and charms of the French language. Over time, I not only achieved a certain facility with the language, but also found some French *copains*.

"But I do wish I had encountered interlocutors as engaging as Linda Phillips Ashour and Claire Lerognon, whose passion for French would have greatly sustained me. For, unlike my teachers at the Sorbonne, they appreciate and celebrate that mastering a language — and life — is not about obsessing on perfection, but about savoring the journey as we go and being prepared to 'learn piecemeal.'"

> — *Peter Skerry, Professor of Political Science at Boston College and Nonresident Senior Fellow at the Brookings Institution*

THE HEART
of an
ARTICHOKE

*A Dialogue à Deux
About French Language,
Literature, and Life*

LINDA PHILLIPS ASHOUR AND CLAIRE LEROGNON

CALEC - TBR Books
New York - Paris

To my mother and her map of the world

— Linda Phillips Ashour

À mon frère Gilles

When Eve walked among
the animals and named them —
nightingale, red-shouldered hawk,
fiddler crab, fallow deer —
I wonder if she ever wanted them
to speak back, looked into
their wide wonderful eyes
and whispered, *Name me, Name me.*

"A Name" by Ada Limón

— Claire Lerognon

Contents

Introduction

LINDA: **How many people do you know who studied French in school or spent a year abroad in college but now regret losing the language they once loved?**

Maybe you're one of them. Your eyes stay glued to the subtitles during a French film. French classes seem scary, expensive, or both. A week in Paris, let alone a year in Provence, seems beyond reach. So what could keep your fervor for the language alive or reignite it after such a long hiatus?

The Heart of an Artichoke offers an informal approach to learning that will help reawaken readers' passion for the language. Our exploration of language, life, and culture is an unconventional alternative to classroom instruction. It mixes the task-based approach that is the backbone of Claire's teaching practice with the piecemeal learning I cobbled together after living almost nine years in France.

In a dialogue that began years ago, I stand in for you, the reader. If you've ever wished you'd asked more questions of your teachers or perhaps challenged the answers, this book allows you that freedom now. As coauthor and friend, I took a lot of liberties with my *professeure*. Not only did Claire encourage my interruptions with grace and good humor, she often turned the tables on me with questions of her own.

It may come as a surprise to you — as it did to me — to learn that mastering grammar and sounding French won't make you fluent. More important than the perfectly constructed sentences Francophiles often crave are communicative *savoir-faire* and intercultural *savoir-être*. Who knew that beginning an exchange, almost any exchange, in French with *bonjour* takes a speaker farther than an impeccably rolled R?

Claire and I debunk a few other comparable myths as we peel back the leaves of the artichoke. Above all, learning a language is learning to communicate — to achieve a purpose. Instead of rules and exercises, try communicating "for real," as I did in a fan letter to a beloved Gallic actor, or brace yourself for a new *registre de langue* with Claire's down and dirty glossary of street *argot*. As you read about our adventures and come up with your own, remind yourself how you got hooked on French in the first place. *Reculer pour mieux sauter.* Sometimes taking a step back really is the way to leap forward.

So what does learning have to do with an artichoke? A nineteenth-century French maxim says it best, "*Cœur d'artichaut, une feuille pour tout le monde*" — heart of an artichoke, a leaf for everyone. There's something fresh for French fanatics to discover on every page.

Claire and I talked, laughed, and anguished about what sometimes seemed like a crazy endeavor, frequently returning to our central metaphor and what it represented for each of us. We knew our answers wouldn't be the same as the ones we began with, *et tant mieux.* No matter how much or how often our opinions diverged, we always agreed that pleasure must remain at the core of an enterprise meant to last a lifetime. ❧

First Things First
Tout d'abord

CLAIRE: **"*Quand je serai grande, je serai maîtresse et j'aurai douze enfants.*"** I imagined living on a farm, unaware of how that many children might affect the vocation I dreamed of as a little girl. At least half of the self-prophecy came true: I have been teaching in various capacities for over twenty years.

That it all began as a way to draw closer to my mother is most certain. I was seven and eight and her pupil in second and third grades. Sharing her with twenty daytime rivals and four siblings at night was hell. She explained to me why she was Maîtresse and not Maman in the classroom, and why she could not call on me as often as she would on others. Our secret understanding soothed my heart, yet I kept raising my finger higher each time she failed to respond. I would sit at her desk at night and open my classmates' *cahiers*, religiously screening for errors I could correct, or hatch lesson plans for my own imaginary pupils.

Improbably, teaching found me again.

In the summer of 1990, I worked for a clothing company in Zurich, selling cheap stuff out of big cardboard boxes in what used to be a porn theater. White neon light shone over the slanted floors scarred by torn-out rows of seats. I shouted shoe and clothing sizes with an encouraging word for hesitant customers in rudimentary Swiss German. I needed the money, but the old town at night turned out to be far more precious to the student I was then. It was in one of its narrow winding streets that I first encountered Herbin. The thick ring of people gathered around him and his band obstructed my view, but I could hear the sound of his tap shoes hitting the cobblestones and the "oohs" and "ahs" that accompanied his performance. The end of his Swiss tour and the beginning of our romance meant I would be bound for New York in the fall of the same year.

October 31, 1990. At JFK Airport, the Indian summer air felt gentle on my skin — a touch of the foreign that did not prepare me for the cultural jolt about to follow: a wild Halloween spectacle roaring on the Lower East Side where Herbin lived. That night, in the eyes of a twenty-three-year-old French country girl and newcomer to America, creatures in feathers, glitter, and heels embodied freedom in every sense. Their emancipation cast a spell on me. A place where I could find and be myself, New York had taken hold of me by the end of my stay — and love affair.

Teaching was less a calling than the way to secure a job in a city smitten with French culture and language. A master's in teaching French as a foreign language, or master *français langue étrangère* (FLE), meant I could satisfy my curiosity for both words and life in the Big Apple. The two years it took to earn the degree were to be my last in France.

In the black-and-white photograph, now yellowed with age, I sit on a disheveled bed with a cigarette in my hand. My hair is between lengths: I am growing out a lifetime of boyish looks. The sun that pours into the room forms a circle of light about me. "To Claire: Become one with the sun." The words on the back of the photo are barely visible. Michael, an art student who lived down the hall in our dormitory at Indiana University, wrote them in pencil before he gave the portrait to me as a souvenir of our friendship.

My first year abroad was as an exchange teaching assistant at IU Bloomington, which provided me with accommodation, tuition-free classes, and a few hundred dollars a month in return for introducing "students to French language and selected aspects of French civilization and culture." The arrangement was my initiation into the real world of teaching.

Although I taught an array of students, most classes comprised two distinct learner types: monolingual students eager for a French experience but deaf to foreign sounds and students attending the acclaimed Jacobs School of Music, graced with finely attuned ears and the motivation to sing French, Italian, and German operas. Differentiated learning looked much better on paper — when it was on paper.

The lesson plan, supplied by the textbook and bible of the Department of French, was the lesson I was not to plan but to unquestionably obey. Each class had been mapped out from beginning to end with set milestones that didn't allow for shortcuts or route changes. The stern approach epitomized the kind of teaching I could not and did not want to do. I thought of my mother's classroom with a pang. The magnificence of trees, the birth of a dragonfly, the spell of foreign accents … everything she made us see and experience would become stories. She had unified a disparate group of immigrants and middle-class Alsatian kids by sharpening our desire for language and capacity for learning it. I longed for the space to build and exercise skills of my own.

It took a few years to find it. Back in the mid-'90s, the Lycée Français de New York was still housed in *beaux arts* townhouses with marble staircases, fireplaces, and ornate ceilings. My students there were four-year-old New Yorkers pressed into learning French by parents in love with *la langue de Molière*. My best and most creative teaching years were spent making French fun and yummy to children playing hide-and-seek in the nooks and crannies of makeshift classrooms. We sang, mimed, and danced vowels and consonants, drew them in the air with sticks and flying ribbons. We built crowns for moms and dads on Mother's and Father's Day, devoured stories and told our own with characters conjured from watercolor stains. The book in which they came to life, *La Reine Louise est revenue!*, gave new meaning to FLE: no longer a *langue étrangère*, French was declared a *langue extraordinaire*.

These children and their progress informed my teaching practice. Reluctant at first, they gradually embraced and learned a language hardly spoken at home or outside of school — lured in by books and crowns. I understood then that creating incentive was a fundamental part of teaching.

This understanding held true as adults replaced children in class. I joined the United Nations Language and Communications Programme (now the Language and Communications Training Unit) in 2002, and with no textbook quite aligned with the needs of the organization's personnel, my colleagues and I agreed it was time to build a curriculum that rose to the challenge. Instructional design called for an *esprit d'équipe*, engineering skills, and pedagogical instincts. Widely held views — one, that communication involves much more than linguistic skills and, two, that languages are best learned when needed — had given rise to the task-based approach that we adopted. Whether to make crowns or carry out an organization's mission, learning always has to have a purpose.

For a good ten years, face-to-face training accounted for most of the teachers' time. Our responsibilities today require teaching in a broader sense. Communication skills courses tailored to specific departments have become in demand, as have blended and online courses to suit the evolving needs of the organization. Even more needed is the promotion of multilingualism in a wider context. Two teacher-led projects brought fame (and one Secretary-General Award) to our program: The new *United Nations Language Framework* harmonizes learning and assessment for the six official languages across the UN Secretariat. New as well, the gender-inclusive language guidelines foster equality, inclusivity, and diversity in the workplace. Project management added breadth to our skills — and a new job title: UN language teachers have today become communication specialists.

In truth, my management skills were tested long before the UN. An altogether different kind of project started soon after I set foot in New York — supporting myself as a freelancer. My memories of this time are mostly visual. Manhattan's roofs made striking *tableaux*. A large water tower loomed over the plain rooms, formerly maids' quarters, where

I met with private students at the French Institute, known today as French Institute Alliance Française (FIAF). Most came for company and a good talk, or a "conversation class," and social skills then were my best asset.

Apartments of private word-of-mouth clients offered other postcard views of Manhattan. A 360-degree panorama of the island, rivers, and bridges left me breathless the first time I toured Kate's Riverside Drive penthouse. Funny, charming Kate, senior writer/producer for a national news network, was plagued with an inability to pronounce the French language. She and I tried everything: endless repetition, role-playing, songs, movies, red wine, and more. What she did very well was throw memorable dinner parties featuring her *cassoulet*, the hearty, meat-studded bean stew that some of her friends (myself included) found as delicious as it was hard to digest.

Tuulikki, on the other hand, was a pro at pronunciation. The view from her apartment gave onto a posh Park Avenue building, though I much preferred gazing at the collection of her own delicate oil paintings hanging on the walls. We spent countless Thursday afternoons munching on nuts and cookies while exchanging personal stories in impeccable French, a language she swallowed whole in the Paris of the '50s. I called her and Perry, her husband of sixty-five years, my adopted grandparents. Balanchine and the New York City Ballet were always a part of our evenings together. By their late eighties, they preferred DVDs and the privacy and comfort of their living room to the live performances we had gone to for many years. Sitting in the front row between the two of them with the cat purring in my lap remains a treasured memory.

Kate and Tuulikki were family while other students became close friends. During my early carefree years in New York, they all put bread and butter on my plate — later on just butter *dans les épinards*, but helping make ends meet wasn't all there was to it. Though I didn't know it then, the convergence of friendship and teaching primed me for a group of women I would teach and learn from for a decade.

"Ma voisine veut se remettre au français. C'est une mordue de grammaire, très sympa … un brin BCBG. Elle cherche des cours privés. Ça t'intéresse?"

Sophie was a part of the administrative team when I taught at the Lycée Français. She handled fiery behavior with patience, grace, and good sense and I trusted her keen eye for people. The portrayal of her neighbor triggered my curiosity and so did the prospect of teaching a grammar addict. Taking her up on the offer proved a very right thing to do. Not only did Katherine straddle the language well and thoughtfully, she was a bundle of enthusiasm for anything French: food, wine, and company of course, but also books, history, politics. What had not been mentioned were her social entrepreneurial skills. Our twosomes soon turned into a small group she brought together for the first time in a French restaurant on the Upper East Side. I strained to gauge the levels and aspirations of the four American women speaking French in that noisy bistro. With strikingly different personalities, skills, and needs, they made an attractive ensemble — two therapists, one writer, and one singer — all enthralled with the music of words. I was in for quite a class.

To this day, the red velvet salon at The Carlyle hotel, where we met each month for the last five years of our decade-long French group, remains the quaintest on my list of classrooms. No blackboard, no projector, not even enough space to write; instead, luxury armchairs and a table crowded with food, drinks, and papers. No textbooks either: French novels and the exercises they inspired me to design framed our course of study. This unusual setting was most suitable for Margot's learning profile: to hear, shape, and absorb oral information is a skill she developed as a singer. Anne's thick notepads vouched for her need to see in order to learn. Katherine took few notes and spoke with amazing precision, the proof of strong analytical abilities and longtime commitment to the language. Linda was the most fluent. The score and lyrics of the French she had heard and eventually spoken for years in a southern French village required only minor rearrangements.

It took us one movie, a few novels and short stories, news articles, dozens of fabulous lunch dates, and occasional drama to eventually find our rhythm. *Bonjour tristesse* marked a turning point in that search. An international best seller that caused a furor in the '60s, it is also a piece in which grammar and plot are interwoven. Françoise Sagan could not have written her novel without using the "if" clauses that sustain the narrative. Young Cécile longs to get rid of the woman who threatens a happy-go-lucky life with her father. Her endless scheming and speculation take place with *si*, giving us an opportunity to do a little speculating of our own. How deliberate were the choices the author had made? Could those passages have been worded otherwise without losing their power? Literature provided us with compelling tools to discuss language. That was all we needed.

LINDA: "What would you think about starting a French group?" Katherine, a new friend, asked when she learned that I had lived in the South of France during the '80s.

Cagnes-sur-Mer, Saint-Paul de Vence, and La Colle sur Loup — my return to the States had signaled an end to all that. Those villages now felt remote, as if they belonged to someone else's life. France belonged to the distant past, I explained to Katherine. I tried — and failed — to remember whether "had lived" took the *plus-que-parfait, imparfait,* or the more familiar *passé composé.*

We had barely entered a new millennium and it was a good time for beginnings, but Katherine's idea caught me off guard. I had moved to New York City to remarry and I missed California, where I'd spent many years raising children and writing novels. I was deeply in love, but there was an infestation of cockroaches in my husband's apartment building and jackhammers on the fire escape outside our bedroom window that began the morning we returned from our honeymoon. The crying jags I conducted in private suggested that I'd be better off keeping California, France, and New York City compartmentalized.

Katherine studied me for a moment before addressing my doubts.

"I know a French woman who lives in my building. She can help us find a teacher."

I thought of my children's composition books and all the tiny squares filled with their careful handwriting. They had worked harder in *l'école primaire* than I had in college. My stomach squeezed shut.

"Great!" I shouted without conviction, struggling to be heard at our table of four. There was a lot of racket in the restaurant, much of it produced by my husband and his sparring partner and friend as they fought about rationalism and somebody named John Searle. I'd never seen two former philosophy students in action and couldn't wait for the check to arrive.

Katherine and I toasted a French group that had acquired a frightening reality with the oaky white wine we both preferred, even though chardonnay had become *déclassé* by New York standards. My new pal didn't know that I had been a middling French student in high school and college. When called upon to speak French in anything resembling a classroom these many years later, performance anxiety often sent me into a dither. I spoke the language best after a cup of strong coffee and half my credibility depended on the general hysteria and hand-waving that came naturally to me when much about French did not. What would she do when she discovered I couldn't write a proper French sentence without breaking into a sweat? That grammar threw me into a state had been my little secret until now.

We were deeply grateful to find The Carlyle hotel. When we'd met in each other's homes, children wandered through their own kitchens, distracting us in their search for a snack. Occasionally a man in a bath towel would appear to interrupt us with a question, and whoever was steaming mussels missed out on the dining table action when Claire, our gazelle of grammar, complimented *un joli barbarisme*. We had become a group of friends as well as students by then, hungry to learn more and learn better — but how? We didn't have an exam to pass as proof that we were getting anywhere. All we had were the small victories that indicated something had soaked in.

Someone at the next table shouted in German and I frowned. By then our French group had become wildly territorial. We'd come to think of that corner of the hotel in Manhattan as our spot, a sophisticated extension of the living rooms and kitchen tables where we first met to participate in an enterprise we hadn't always been able to name. Now we huddled together in *notre coin* each month, plumping the cushions along the *banquette* until we settled in to pore over French novels and short story collections. We spent hours there, grousing when guests talked too loudly or invaded our turf in other ways.

"Bonjour, Mesdames. Vous allez bien?"

The manager greeted us warmly, but didn't linger. He was from Brittany, and I would have loved to pummel him with questions about a coast I longed to visit, but his professionalism kept me from getting sloppy. Besides, I didn't want to push my luck.

We took turns inviting Claire each time and asked for individual bills to avoid the confusion of splitting the tab. Ours was not an easy table and we sometimes had special requests. When I declined a glass of champagne on somebody's birthday, our waiter surprised me with ginger ale in a flute glass. He spoke French too and raised his eyebrows at a book jacket he considered *risqué*. Sometimes guests wandered over to ask what we were reading or pushed a bashful child forward to address us in French.

Little girls in frilly dresses flooded Bemelmans Bar next door. The piano player belted out their favorite songs in the saloon where the author of the *Madeline* series painted his famous murals in exchange for a room, but these raucous good times sometimes got the best of us. Anne got up before we finished our exercise.

"Mes amies, il faut que je vous quitte," she sighed.

I wondered how a doctor with a busy practice kept her life in balance with a blended family that included six college-aged children. She tightened the belt on her trench coat and gave each of us a kiss goodbye. Someday I would ask to borrow a few of her French books, but not because I didn't own them myself. She made family trees for our more complicated novels, the only thing she loved better than a good Greek tragedy was Proust, and I was pretty sure the dense notes in Anne's margins were of a much higher order than mine.

French group was over, but not finished. I got home and tried to calm down before I blasted into my husband's study, full of questions about a point of grammar I still couldn't grasp or some subtle understanding that had escaped me until that afternoon. My brief exposure to college-level French often collided with his, and that day I couldn't read my own handwriting as it trailed off the last page of a Moleskine, not that it mattered. The excited gibberish would fade and become something else. On optimistic days, I was even hopeful that it would become something more.

Cœur d'artichaut, une feuille pour tout le monde. Our group was the quintessential artichoke. I can't speak for the others, but I occasionally pricked my fingers and questioned the enterprise, especially in the beginning. The longer we kept at it, however, the closer we got to the heart with ample leaves for everyone. Our tastes and preferences varied wildly. We began by reading from a suggestion box of ideas that reflected Katherine's interest in politics or Anne's taste for classicism. I haunted my local newsstand for articles or short stories that might suit our eclectic tastes and levels of proficiency. Before discovering The Carlyle we advanced by fits and starts each month, alternately watching a film or a tugboat chugging past an apartment overlooking the East River in the discussion that followed. There was talk of playing the movie again to focus on key scenes, an idea we never revived. We read a difficult novel by Marguerite Duras and gave part of Rousseau's *Confessions* a shot, but not until *Bonjour tristesse* did we embrace a book unanimously. For Margot, whose Belgian mother taught French in the New York City public school system, its completion was one of the highlights of her forties.

The lavish hotel wasn't a classroom, but you couldn't have told me that then. The ideal course in my mind would have made any sensible administrator laugh out loud. First things first with a warm-up *dictée* of the sort popularized by Bernard Pivot, the esteemed French journalist and television host who has championed literature and culture for decades. Feeling more alive to the language after the *orthographe*

workout, we would move on to slippery points of grammar taught anecdotally, with a story to reinforce every rule. Like Katherine, I would remember a restaurant in Paris where a fellow diner studied his menu and chose *la viande* rather than *de la viande*, locking in a rule about definite articles by demonstration. Forget textbooks. My scraps of paper and scrambled notes would be stitched together into a chapbook unlocking the mysteries of French connectors once and for all. The final exam would be administered by verbal speed freak Julien Lepers, the former host of *Questions pour un champion* on TV5. Best of all, I would deliver answers in flawless French, thus confirming the net worth of such unconventional studies. Seemingly unrelated fragments would at last be made whole.

One morning I found a pile of index cards inside a tangle of blankets and pillows. *Désormais, désormais, désormais.* I'd written the single word nine times on one of the cards in hopes of remembering that it means "from now on," not to be confused with *néanmoins*, a word that appeared eleven times on the flip side of the card. A curled yellow Post-it revealed another mnemonic strategy. If I grouped troublesome words and sentences together with the novels in which they appeared, would my retention improve? I envisioned the chain-smoking friend of the main character in *La petite fille de Monsieur Linh* as I read his description on another card: "*M. Bark fume toujours autant, peut-être même davantage si tant est que cela soit possible.*"

I stared at the elaborate grammatical structure. The words had become less impermeable over time, but the phrase was hardly something that would ever roll off my tongue — *si tant est que cela soit possible.* There was the damn subjunctive popping up again and I wasn't even sure I knew what the construction meant. I added more butter to my toast and bit down hard.

"Do you think I'll ever master this stuff?"

My husband had nearly made it to his study. "Depends on what you mean by mastery," he said with a heavy sigh.

He wandered off, momentarily free of the giddy enthusiasm and self-doubt that marked my engagement with the French language. If I were truly serious, wouldn't I have hunkered down in a language lab, instead of eating lunch in a fancy hotel with four friends? I wondered what I could truthfully say I learned after reading all those French books. And how did that learning take place?

I pushed aside a chipped cereal bowl and made a new index card, copying the reflections of an erudite *concierge* on reading Kant while eating a cherry plum. For one delicious moment I, too, was leading a life of the mind and of the senses. ❧

Great Expectations
Sans un couac

LINDA: I hope Dickens will forgive us for appropriating his title, but I had, and continue to have, some pretty outlandish misconceptions about learning a language. Some dreams take a long time to fade. I would still love to speak *sans un couac*. What are your thoughts on the subject, Claire?

C Any *couacs* at all — or just the grammar blunders I've always known you to fear and loathe?

L All of the above. Today much of my "immersion" in French comes in the form of the Internet, TV, and movies. Its availability is something worth remembering when I start whining about how I can't pop over to France more often to speak, hear, and live the language. Defining a *couac* now as a *fausse note* gives my blunders a slight upgrade. But when I first lived in France and picked up the language through everyday interactions, a *couac* suggested the honking noise a duck makes. I was intent on sounding like a native, even though I wasn't sure what that meant.

C I can't say I ever yearned to sound American — or British when I lived in London, although the vain girl in me would rather be asked "what country" than "what part of France" she is from. My French accent ranges from discernible to feather-light and blends with lively notes of British and Noo Yawk English. The result is a volatile, flavorful brew, which I've grown to like. So I'm curious: Why were you so determined to sound French?

L Thank you for bringing up vanity, which had plenty to do with it. I may also have been trying to honor a hero of mine back in Oklahoma. Whatever modest foundation I have in French came from a high school teacher who lured me into learning a little something concrete. Mme Krumme was the epitome of no-nonsense chic in her short-sleeved black turtleneck and straight skirt. Her super-short graying hair signaled something radically opposed to the lacquered hairdos of her colleagues. A crisp, clipped pronunciation and sparkling eyes suggested intellectual energy, a large and largely exciting life. She was an exigent teacher and I tested poorly, earning a solid string of Bs. I adored her, but yearned for the whole shebang, which meant a life outside the classroom, any classroom.

C Your portrait of Mme Krumme brings up a question I've been toying with as we embark on this chapter. How much do "sounding" and "looking" have in common? My once-cool Brooklyn neighborhood has borne the brunt of Frenchification in recent years. As I walk its streets and look at the people, I catch myself thinking, "They're French" before I can hear them. No berets, no *baguettes*, not even hairy legs or outward elegance — can the world please move on? — but a *je ne sais quoi* in the way they carry themselves, interact with friends, spouses, children … A hint of the familiar that can't be reproduced — contrary to sounds or rhythms.

"DÉJEUNER DU MATIN"

Il a bu le café au lait
Et il a reposé la tasse
Sans me parler

L I memorized Jacques Prévert's "Déjeuner du matin" along with every other high schooler whose concept of French was romance freighted with sadness and a cup of robust coffee with hot milk. It remains a classroom favorite if student videos on YouTube are any indication. A quick sampling turns up the same simple props: mug or cup, spoon, and sullen, silent guy. But what better exposure to the *passé composé* than this perennial by a writer *Le Figaro* called "*le plus parisien des poètes*"?

L Looking, sounding, and even being someone different was all of a piece my freshman year in college. French signified sophistication and nothing appealed to me more. Desperately homesick and too proud to admit it, I discovered existential literature and Mateus Rosé, a potent combination. Did it matter that the wine was produced

I GET WHAT YOU'RE SAYING

L   If we are to believe the many books and articles on French women and *le style français*, it transcends knowing what to do with a scarf or how to eat with gusto while remaining thin, both of which Joyce Wadler lampooned in an article for the *New York Times* in 2012. After the article ran, a dozen of the twenty-one comments that followed expressed outrage at infractions ranging from spelling errors to insensitivity to cultural nuance, and "a completely silly and fictitious notion of national identity (American vs. French), which doesn't ever exist in reality."

Wadler did nail it, though, when her fictitious Frenchwoman lets her American interlocutor have it. "'*Roi, roi, roi!*' she screamed. 'It is a simple word! Why can none of you pronounce it?'" Who wouldn't argue that the French R can be as elusive as French *panache*?

in Portugal? Probably not. It was sweet, cheap, and the stately buildings on the label looked Mediterranean if you didn't know better. Sartre, Camus, and Nietzsche had a heady effect. I smoked menthol cigarettes until I was sick to my stomach and wrote about life being a *comédie* in journals I've only had the courage to look at recently. Have I just stumbled into beret and *baguette* land?

C   I'll give you a pass. You were young.

L   And bored silly after one semester of French taught by a professor with jet-black hair who looked like Stanley Tucci. There wasn't a thing wrong with his teaching, but I didn't want grammar instruction. I wanted the French life of the mind suggested by photographs of Simone de Beauvoir et al. at Les Deux Magots. I wanted to suffer because suffering was romantic, but only if I could have a good time doing it. The shockingly sunny themes of "Le tourbillon de la vie" in *Jules et Jim* were an inspiration. After seeing the film, my discordant version of the Parisian life of the mind nearly always took place at the beach.

C   Movies threw us both for a loop. Only I had no idea I'd be living in Brooklyn a year after I watched *Do the Right Thing*. The summer of

JULES ET JIM

L   It's astonishing that "Le tourbillon de la vie," which perfectly captures the romantic vicissitudes of Catherine, Jules, and Jim, was composed well before the film was made. Three men, each of whom has been either her lover or husband, are enraptured by Jeanne Moreau's performance of the song in Truffaut's 1962 New Wave masterpiece. If Catherine harbors any misgivings about the emotional havoc she wreaks, you would never know it as she sings this insouciant and unsettling song to her admirers.

> *Quand on s'est connu, quand on s'est reconnu*
>
> *Pourquoi s'perdre de vue, se reperdre de vue?*
>
> *Quand on s'est retrouvé, quand on s'est réchauffé*
>
> *Pourquoi se séparer?*

Serge Rezvani, an actor in the film as well as the composer of the song, revealed that the song poked fun at Moreau and her former husband, the actor and director Jean-Louis Richard, in an interview with Europe1 after her death in 2017. "*Ils se sont mariés, ils se séparaient, puis ils se remettaient ensemble. J'ai écrit cette chanson pour me moquer d'eux.*" Not only did he succeed in teasing his friends, Rezvani got to strum along on his guitar in a film that has fascinated legions of film critics and fans ever since.

1991, my first in New York, matched Spike Lee's portrayal of the city: hot — and not just weather hot. It was youth all over again.

L   I, on the other hand, was in a hurry to leave my youth behind. Being a mother was one step in the right direction, but I wanted to speed up the process once I had the good fortune to move from California to France. My children would eventually hoist heavy *cartables* onto their backs and trudge off to school. On a certain level I envied them. School and early babysitters gave them an advantage over their mom's unscripted approach to learning. I was wild to sound French and as urbane as the language I heard around me, but how to accomplish this? Cagnes-sur-Mer in 1979 offered salient possibilities.

C   Wild to sound like a Parisian or a Cagnoise?

L   Paris couldn't have been farther away. Clues about how French could or should be spoken came with a distinctly southern accent. I learned that a furnished house came furnished with people too. Stella Bouvet, youngest daughter of next-door neighbors protected by an iron fence and a pack of fierce guard dogs, presented herself the first week we arrived and shyly explained she was my *femme de ménage*. One day when Savannah and I were in the garden, an enormous snake slithered past. I shrieked and grabbed my child and ran to Stella's house where there were always men sitting around outside, dismantling machines or playing cards. Blind instinct suggested at least one of them would know what to do with a garden that was Eden no more.

"*Au fusil!*" the elder Bouvet cried, dashing inside for his shotgun.

Their speaking style was very different from the painstaking delivery of the landlord who lived beneath us with his son. Gone were carefully carved syllables, each one neat and distinct from the other. Their French was difficult to understand, whereas our landlord's enunciation sounded perfect to my untrained ears. My desire to sound French definitely didn't mean sounding like the Bouvet family. How about the accents where you grew up?

C   Accents are markers of class. Only people comfortable with, or proud of, their social backgrounds would want to sound like the Bouvets.

What Prime Minister Jean Castex may be most remembered for is his southwestern inflection. Not until he took office in 2020 did a French public figure speak with a distinct accent. I remember being surprised when former president François Hollande stepped — slipped? — outside of his usual French. Interviewed in his native Corrèze, he talked about *le café du village* with a southern lilt, a mere whisper compared to the Bouvets' roar, but enough to tell he had let his guard down — and loved the place.

To answer your question, I'd say the "Alsatian Bouvets" speak a French that blasts thick consonants and long, winding vowels. Add a few structural *couacs* — direct imports from the German dialect spoken in Alsace — and you understand why they're easy targets for accent impersonators.

L   I will forever think of you as a mountain girl, no matter how many years you've lived in New York. How deeply embedded is the dialect?

C   I can sound Alsatian — convincingly for a minute or two. My mother insisted only French be spoken at home. As talented young adults, both my parents outgrew their working-class peers and shortcomings with the language. But four years under German occupation and dialect-speaking households were obstacles many did not overcome. Mom once told me about a five-year-old boy in the kindergarten class she taught in 1954, the first in her long career. Dazzled by his *maîtresse*'s red lips on one of the rare mornings she wore lipstick, he exclaimed, *"Rouge bouche aujourd'hui!"* — three words that moved and disheartened her. They showed the skills of a two-year-old and the struggle Alsatian kids experienced learning the language of their own country.

UNE HISTOIRE PAS COMME LES AUTRES

C   The object of a tug-of-war between France and Germany, Alsace changed hands four times in recent history, from 1870 to 1945, and was French for only a third of those seventy-five years. My parents' generation, born in the 1930s of parents who had been German citizens, spoke the dialect — an offspring of the German spoken in southern Germany — as their native tongue. The little French they spoke as children — a mere act of defiance towards the World War II occupiers — never grew strong enough to dethrone *l'alsacien*. They entered adult life proud French citizens but foreigners to the French language.

L   Your anecdote surprises me. I've seen the Alsacienne Claire on rare occasions and then only for comic effect. Does this self emerge after conversations with your family?

C   Not after, during — usually morning calls on my way to work, when Dad's impromptu *"Sàlü dü, geht's?"* sets the tone. We're off to small, sweet talk that my *couacs* won't spoil, on the contrary. It is as if breaking into the "secret language" he spoke when I was a little girl pleading for translation gives us a new chance today. I wonder: Could our dialect help put into words what lies unsaid between us? *Mais je m'éloigne …*

MOUNTAIN GIRL

C My name is pronounced and spelled the same way as the *entrée* it takes guts to order in French restaurants. It is written as one word and not two: We are not descended from French nobility, not even, as is often asked, from a family of butchers. Nor are we big meat eaters, although we famously ventured, time and again, in the mountains of the Hautes-Vosges where the Schaffhausers' farm was nestled. Their handmade *fromage de Munster* was divine and often diverted us from the hiking trail that meandered behind the farm. They also sold meat, but only to people they knew well and trusted, for they sold it "illegally," bypassing health regulations and taxation. The young calves were slaughtered on the farm in the heart of winter and the meat cut into big chunks in the barn. A call from our friends, and we'd drive up the mountain pass, park the car at the top, put backpacks on and ski to the farm, gliding through fir forests and across windblown lands. At the barn few

words were exchanged as meat was packed and schnapps, rounds of it, warmed up bodies and souls. Night had fallen by the time we would leave, and the little girl I was proudly followed in her dad's tracks, giddy with excitement and the weight of a bloody secret strapped on her shoulders.

Back to the comic in me. The Alsatian drawl does spice things up when the class goes silent for too long. But I mainly switch accents (my repertoire also includes Swiss and Canadian French) to introduce sounds and rhythms students are rarely exposed to. Most of what they hear is close to "standard" French — an adjective I use reluctantly.

L By standard French do you mean the kind I might hear on a TV5 news broadcast?

NO LONGER UNCOOL

C The twenty-four *langues régionales* spoken on French territory are back in fashion. The Basque, Breton, Catalan, Corsican, and Occitan dialects are taught to the young and old and learned in school by a growing number of students. Street names — even checkbooks — are written in both French and the local vernacular in regions where ardent activists claim the right to a fuller cultural identity. The fight against cultural extinction is a trendy one for politicians to lead, and former president Hollande's reversal of his promise to ratify the European Charter for Regional or Minority Languages caused disappointment and anger amongst advocates.

C TV5Monde actually does the best job showcasing the francophone world today. TF1 or France 2 or 3, however, feature the French spoken in the Région Centre-Val de Loire, known as the "cradle of the French language." The Loire River that runs through it served for centuries as a linguistic frontier. North of it was *langue d'oïl* territory, south, *langue d'oc* — both *oc* and *oïl* mean "yes" in the two vernaculars. The further away from the river, the less they had in common. It is, not surprisingly, still true of regional accents today. The residents of Lille, the most northerly city, near the Belgian border, and those of Ajaccio in Corsica can sound as if they are speaking different languages.

L Would you say native Parisians sound "standard," that term you use with reluctance? And how does the rest of France feel about that?

C More so than their southern and northern *concitoyens,* yet their accents are joked about just as much. Snooty Parisians are the laughingstock of the rest of France; some even become literary material. Muriel Barbery's *L'élégance du hérisson* takes place in an *hôtel particulier*

EDDY BELLEGUEULE

C *Une belle gueule* is a good-looking guy, and spelled as one word, a common last name in northern France, which Édouard Louis decided to break away from. "Eddy Bellegueule is the name my parents gave me when I was born. It sounds dramatic," the new literary star said in an interview with *The Paris Review*, "but yes, I wanted to kill him — he wasn't me, he was the name of a childhood I hated."

In his debut novel, *En finir avec Eddy Bellegueule*, Louis shows a world that was never shown before, a world so hidden it was made invisible. The reality of Hallencourt, the "provincial hell" he grew up in, came as a shock to many: "*Un territoire de bouseux racistes, sexistes et homophobes qui se mouchent dans leurs doigts et meurent d'alcool et de gangrène.*"

The young writer shook the literary scene not only because of what he says but how he says it, with two languages intertwined throughout the book: the narrator's *language bourgeois, normalien* — Louis attended the illustrious École normale supérieure — and the Bellegueules' vernacular, "*le language de l'exclusion, des déshérités.*" "*Faire du littéraire avec du non-littéraire,*" as he often stated, compels the reader to see — and hear — the social outcasts of twenty-first-century France — a new literary strand he named "*littérature de la confrontation.*"

I wonder whether young Eddy Bellegueule spoke with *l'accent ch'ti* or the much lighter inflection still coloring Édouard Louis's speech today. And whether sounding northern will help reunite the two.

of the chic *seizième arrondissement,* where a not so chic *concierge* tends to the residents. The exaggerated vowels, "hissed" words, and pitch variations characteristic of their *accent pointu* are best embodied by Mâdâme Rosen who "always talks as if she had a cockroach in her mouth." Renée Michel, the *concierge* and star of the novel, avoids her like the plague. Why this avid reader, thinker, and *grande dame* of language hides her literary light is the mystery that unfolds over the course of the book. I wouldn't be surprised if the accent of Belleville, spoken by Parigots (native working-class Parisians) and sung by Edith Piaf, where a *concierge* is a *conciarge* with a rolled R and open A, were part of her disguise.

L   What would Renée have made of the mannered French that surfaced when one of our guests in Cagnes began reciting poetry to his uncomfortable audience at the end of a raucous American Thanksgiving? He was notable for his fur coat, his dismay at tea that had steeped too long, and diction that suggested advanced degrees from big-city universities. His pinched and vaguely pained delivery suggested it was not meant for a mere mortal like myself.

Later I could pick up its echoes the evening of our first dinner in a French home. When the attention turned to cuisine, our delightful older host swiveled around on the fancy settee in his living room, thrilled that I agreed with him. A thin slice of cold butter melting over hot green beans *was* one of the finest delicacies on earth. He praised my husband's French and began to flatter my own with a preposition that I will never forget.

L'ÉLÉGANCE DU HÉRISSON

L   *L'élégance du hérisson* was published by Gallimard in 2006, becoming a best seller the following year. Eventually translated into over forty languages and adapted for film, this novel evokes philosophy, popular culture, and French class structure in language that moves from dense to accessible right along with the protagonist. We'll have more to say about Renée and her entourage later.

"Quant à Madame ..."

His voice trailed off into an admiring statement or two full of golden swirls and flourishes. This was fancy French for a fancy evening. Experiences like this remain my favorite form of learning. For some time they've felt like something I could inhabit, as if they were a country.

C   Did you succeed?

L   I was keen on speaking the most convincing French I could. But I was clearly a resident of two worlds. My son spent his toddler years in cowboy boots from Oklahoma and I even sported my own — in red. Once in a while someone would compliment my French, which was pure catnip. I wanted more words, more language, more everything, though how to acquire them remained a problem. I wanted to come by language the way Savannah did, through relationships. Friendships of my own would come later. I had enough sense to understand that without them, both dinner party French and the kind with a shotgun slung over its shoulder were more than I could manage. I set my sights on something more accessible, like the children's magazines I bought for the kids. Television was an option, but programming in those years made it challenging.

C   Is that how you got hooked on television? As a way to absorb the language?

L   It was a start. There was no television broadcasting before noon when we first arrived in

PRESIDENTIAL FANCY

C   On May 8, 2017, France elected its youngest president and fanciest talker — and with Emmanuel Macron, nothing's too fancy. Take the closing election debate, for example. He served the *coup de grâce* to Marine Le Pen's presidential hopes in a French seasoned with rare ingredients — 1 *saut de cabri*, 1 *galimatias*, 1 *antienne*, 1 *broutard* — and, rarer still, some finely aged *poudre de perlimpinpin*. Some may find his way with language *désuet*, but I will always choose *perlimpinpin* over the notorious *"Casse-toi, pauvre con!"* of his predecessor.

France, and the news programs that followed left me cold. But my moratorium on television ended when I got my first taste of Bernard Pivot, the grocer's son from Lyon whose literary talk show *Apostrophes* delighted and informed television audiences during the '70s and '80s. The hank of dark hair that fell over his forehead as he grew more animated about literature, a fervor for books and their authors that literally brought him to the edge of his seat — I was smitten. And determined to understand what this literary crusader was talking about.

C   He was, and is, a national treasure — still very much in the game via Twitter, weighing in on everything from politics and the *argot* of the rich and the poor to his beloved *matchs de foot*.

L   I followed the show with reverence and regularity. Pivot was living the life of the mind in Technicolor. I figured if I could capture one word out of twenty, I was ahead. Mostly I worked on familiarity with Pivot's cadence, the rise and fall of his wonderful words. I leafed through the books he discussed when I could find them at the commercial center

VOISINAGE

L   My daughter called out for her best friend, Deborah, several times a day after our move to Cagnes and drew pictures of California at our massive dining table, but she wouldn't be lonely for long. Savannah would soon find her own *entrée* into French language and culture.

A few steps beyond our house stood a bustling cottage with a front door that was always open. A deeply tanned older woman worked in the garden as parents dressed for the office dropped off children of various ages. When the sun rose higher in the sky, she would remove her blouse and lie down on her chaise as children swarmed around her with garden tools and sand shovels. She berated a *petit monstre*, and clambered up a ladder to prune a fruit tree. Adoring children called her Mamie.

One day I summoned up my courage and rang the bell at the gate. All smiles and thoroughly unapologetic, Mme Chalopin approached in her bra and straight blue skirt. Could Savannah come and play with the others for an hour? I asked if she would let me pay her and she waved me off, saying we would *discuter* later.

The garden was empty when I rang the bell on Mme Chalopin's gate.

"Entrez, entrez!"

near the Nice airport where I shopped for groceries and savored a *croque monsieur* made with real *béchamel*. I trusted that the rest would come later and for the most part, it did. This all took time, though, and I was in a hurry to plunge in. Are your students in a similar rush to sound French?

C   No. Sounding French won't make much of a difference when interacting with the populations and dignitaries of Mali or Haiti or whichever French-speaking country they go to on field missions. But effective communication skills will, and they require a host of abilities including clear pronunciation — not necessarily a French accent.

L   I've always equated the two. To speak with a good French accent is to have good pronunciation.

I approached the house gingerly through a maze of potted plants.

"*Savannah, elle est là ta maman.*"

Her name sounded more graceful with the even emphasis on all syllables. It sounded, well, French. My daughter sat at a communal kitchen table, hard at work on a *baguette* the length of her forearm smeared with butter and jam. The biggest Mason jar I had ever seen stood in the middle of the table and the children took turns scooping out their portion of jam. Savannah, every syllable sounding, helped herself again and smiled.

Nothing could have prepared me for the day a couple of months after meeting Mamie when my little girl turned to me at the gate and told me to go away.

"*Vous êtes partie et d'un coup elle a commencé à me parler en français!*"

Mme Chalopin delivered the news, proudly holding Savannah in her arms. My daughter wasn't about to trot out her new language in front of me. She had been storing up vocabulary, wisely waiting for the opportune moment to strut her stuff. "Mommy, are we in French or in English?" When her skills in both languages later solidified, she would answer this question for herself.

C   Correct. But the reverse is not true. Clear pronunciation can — and usually will — come with a foreign accent. I am the perfect example of that, and make it clear to students from the start. As long as they don't obstruct the flow, foreign accents are charming — and stubborn. There's no getting rid of them entirely unless you travel back in time to become a child again.

L   I'm convinced, although I will always be drawn to impeccable-sounding French. Think moth to a flame.

C   Keep flaunting those French Rs, just don't inflate their importance. ❦

The Glitter of Grammar
Une règle d'or

LINDA: **Concentrating on accents and pronunciation gradually gave way to obsessing about *les fautes de grammaire*.** How to achieve even the slightest degree of mastery? Grammar books that are gathering dust on the shelf glower at me, offended by a question with such an obvious answer. I could reach for *Advanced French Grammar*, by Monique L'Huillier, purchased in a spasm of ambition, or a more recent acquisition touted as *"La grammaire qui aime les écrivains."* Nevertheless, *Le petit bon usage de la langue française,* a contemporary update and homage to the esteemed Maurice Grevisse, threw this writer into despair.

C It might be time to reexamine those intentions.

L When I returned to California after my '80s sojourn in France, I spoke little French, consumed as I was by the responsibilities of single parenthood, writing, and teaching. French was relegated to the back burner. Had it not been for my move to New York, a new marriage, and our French group at The Carlyle, what remnants of language remained might well have disappeared. My focus took a drastic turn. Monthly meetings at the storied hotel and reading literature I'd never had the time or impulse to explore in France meant trying to trot out fancy French in earnest. Was it fun? Yes. Did it corrupt the enterprise? A bit.

I grew awfully fussy in the pursuit of — what? Delicious details like what the ghostly *accent circonflexe* represents, a letter that is no longer there. A whole missing history under one roof-shaped symbol, who could resist exploring that? But agonizing over grammar didn't work miracles, as you well know. I even became self-conscious about the French I had learned under fire and hyperaware of making mistakes, relative pronouns being one of my most common errors. The failure to finesse and refine a workable French when I had the relative freedom to do so was often an uninvited guest at my party.

C This may come as news to you, but your fantasies and delusions about grammar are common among learners. Many think of it as the be-all, end-all of language and even more expect to be able to "trot out fancy French" by just attending classes — or French groups.

Grammar became our focus because it was the easy way out. Beyond our fascination with the subject, we had, after all, little choice but to rejoice in intellectual pursuit. With disparate levels and time constraints — three hours a month including small talk and sumptuous lunch breaks — only magic would have enabled the four of you to develop seamless language skills. Mistaking high-end grammar sessions for the road to flawless French "corrupted your enterprise" more than the fancy sentences we examined. *Le subjonctif imparfait* may not be *monnaie courante* in everyday French, *j'en conviens*, but much of the grammar we dug up from the novels we read is. Only we kept unearthing tools we didn't have time to hone — and ten years of reading amounted to an impressive collection that, just like your grammar books on their bookshelf, gathered dust in the red velvet salon at The Carlyle.

COCASSERIE

L I once picked up a postcard in Paris advertising a play I would never see. The charming artwork featured a fish in a tree, but I clung to it for a critic's blurb with shades of meaning that multiplied upon each rereading. "*La langue française est servie avec subtilité et cocasserie.*" Language that is simultaneously subtle and farcical? Sign me up. I wanted to be the smart buffoon speaking sonorous, subtle French, and still do. *Cocasserie.* What a great word. I fall for the whole business again, as foolish as that fish in a tree.

DES POISSONS
DANS LES ARBRES
Texte et mise en scène d'Alexis Voriget-Wahl
PASCAL   ALEX
AUBERT   WALTZ

Locations Fnac - Carrefour
0 892 68 36 22 (0.34€/mn) - www.fnac.com

L Maybe it was *une folie*, but those were heady moments. Being able to identify *le subjonctif imparfait* and understanding for one brief moment why it was being used in a particular passage was fascinating. Sadly, the information didn't stick, nor did much of the other grammar we examined, but I enjoyed the digressions.

C Remember twelve-year-old Paloma, Renée's brainy little friend in *L'élégance du hérisson*? Her take on grammar was ours then: "To do grammar is to dissect language, to see it naked and realize how inventive, solid, rich, and subtle it is." Never before had grammar been given the limelight — or sparked a romance. No wonder we treasured the novel.

PALOMA

C Language and its *jolies tournures* play a key role in shaping the singular friendship between Renée and Paloma. Born the youngest daughter of a family as vain as she is perceptive, the eccentric twelve-year-old and second narrator in the two-voice novel describes grammar as a path to beauty, what she tracks down to make life, as absurd as she says it is, worth living.

L Renée and Monsieur Ozu's was a very literary love affair.

C He had just moved into the building and Mâdâme Rosen — the one who speaks as if she has a cockroach in her mouth — introduces him to Renée while alluding to the neighbors' uncleaned doormat.

"Le paillasson qui était devant la porte des Arthens n'a pas été nettoyé. Pouvez-vous pallier à ça?"

A demand as rude as it is ungrammatical — *pallier*, unbeknownst to many native speakers, does not take a preposition. When the mistake jars them both, Monsieur Ozu realizes the "illiterate" *concierge* is anything but. All at once the jig is up, jump-starting a courtship grounded in grammar. A tale written just for you ...

L It's a comfort to know that even native speakers make errors, but all this over a misplaced *à*? It will come as no surprise that I tried to beg off when a friend asked me to write to the CEO of a French boutique

THE WALKING WOUNDED

L Bescherelle ta mère is *faute*-finding at its irreverent best. The website exposes spelling and grammatical mistakes made on television, in newspapers, and even in supermarkets. Sylvain Szewczyk has followed up with a book called *Je t'apprends le français, bordel!* His mission is bold and he's often funny, but I wonder whether Anne-Marie Gaignard is laughing.

If Gaignard's experience as a child is any measure, feeling like a *cancre*, or dunce, means you spend most of your time as one of the walking wounded who are terrorized by words. She was told she was dyslexic and sent to a speech therapist as a child, but her difficulties with reading and spelling persisted. And the scholastic stigma doesn't necessarily end with graduation. New to the workforce after having survived the trauma of *dictées* and being perpetually lost in a *forêt de mots*, she was chided by a salesperson for her misspelling of the number *quatre-vingt-neuf* (it does sound like *œuf*) when she wrote out a check for a blouse. To find out later, after attending a conference on dyslexia at age thirty-six, that she wasn't dyslexic after all was life-changing.

Gaignard has gone to bat with a vengeance for struggling learners. My copy of *La revanche des nuls en orthographe* has arrived and who knows? Maybe her approach to spelling and grammar issues is just the ticket for this non-native writer.

about opening up a store in Los Angeles. I explained I didn't have the skills for the job, but she persisted. I can report that every sentence in my email was Googled through and through, down to the "*Cordialement, Linda Phillips Ashour.*"

C Not just a misplaced *à*. Ever read Hans Christian Andersen's *La princesse au petit pois*? Made to sleep on twenty mattresses with a single pea beneath them all, a young woman wakes up "black and blue all over her body." No one but a real princess could be so delicate. Well, *pallier à* is to grammar what the pea is to the princess: a royal test. Only those bruised by it belong to nobility.

A SINGING CURE

C　Dear Walking Wounded,

Will you please accept a musical attempt at cheering you up?

Let me start by introducing Rebecca Manzoni — or, rather, by quoting François Busnel as he welcomed her onto the set of *Si on lisait*, his show dedicated to "*les plus beaux textes de la littérature et de la chanson françaises*": "*Notre experte en grammaire vous réveille chaque matin vers 7h20, 7h22 sur l'antenne de France Inter avec ce que j'appelle une véritable bulle de poésie en musique.*" Every morning indeed, Manzoni's fresh, delightful prose on music takes you far and wide through the world of songs.

Now prepare for her special musical tour — one designed just for you, my wounded friends. An homage to errors in French songs, because even the most beautiful lyrics have mistakes, sung loud and clear.

"*Pas besoin d'avoir le nez dans le Bescherelle pour écrire une bonne chanson,*" says Manzoni, and rightfully so. In one short sentence and with all his heart, Jean Yanne makes two monstrous blunders: "*Si tu t'en irais ... je crois bien que je mourirais.*" Renaud has another killer pair: "*Dès que le vent soufflera, je repartira. Dès que les vents tourneront, nous nous en allerons.*" Alain Bashung rounds off in style with yet one more lame future tense: "*Un jour je t'aimerai moins ... un jour je courirai moins, jusqu'au jour où je ne courirai plus ...*"

So, what say you, Walking Wounded? These guys twist conjugation for rhyme and meter's sake. You make earnest blunders and don't get away with it — let alone praised. But just listen to Bashung's answer when asked about his deliberate glitch: "*Une chanson n'est pas faite pour donner des leçons de français, au contraire, j'ai de la tendresse pour tous ceux qui font des maladresses. Vivent les émus*" ... and long live the clumsy, those who get carried away by a melody.

If the most famous tripped for swing and flow, you, dear Walking Wounded, are allowed anything that will carry your French away.

Most sincerely,

Claire

PREMIÈRES DICTÉES

C The elaborate striped thing to the left of Valérie must be the *pomme* she looks so happy to eat. Does the prickly garnish on top compensate for the missing O and upset E in the word I was transcribing from memory for the very first time? No doubt *zéro faute* was already my standard in first grade. My *cahiers* are testimonies to the discipline of dictation, an exercise we practiced daily to enter the magical — and densely populated — world of spelling and grammar. By the end of the school year, my vowels looked solid and trim but my T's had yet to be crossed.

But more important is your email — for that is precisely how to improve your written skills: communicate "for real" as opposed to combing the *Advanced French Grammar* for rules and exercises. Don't get me wrong, your copy could use a light dusting, but if you're short on time — or motivation — "Googling through and through" is worth its weight in grammar. Studying a language as a system, understanding how it works, is a very good thing; bringing this knowledge to life in interactions is another endeavor altogether — think heart of an artichoke, each leaf a writing workout.

L Too bad there's no way to autocorrect one's own speech. It must drive you nuts when I ask you to point out my mistakes, but don't feel singled out: I often ask French friends and even strangers to do the same thing. Why preface conversations this way? I suspect it's less a learning tool than a way of saving face. I can keep my sentences short, choppy, and correct or dare *ce dont* or *desquelles* if my audience knows they're in for a mistake or two. These invitations to instruct often yield real treasures, especially from friends who are as keen on proper usage as I am. Mostly they function as a safety net, emboldening me to explore more ambitious sentences or use structures I've heard, but don't always understand.

   C I can't help but notice that your requests for corrections morphed into invitations to instruct. Whether conscious or not, this shift in words reveals a shift in perception, which is that errors make learning stick. I'm a firm believer in mutual corrections, provided mistakes are accepted — and valued — for what they are: the opportunity to gain a deeper, finer understanding of language. *Alors, convaincue?*

LEARNING THE LINGO

   L Duolingo is an online language course that uses the carrot and stick approach to learning a foreign language. Currently lingots, a form of virtual currency, and a triumphant blast of trumpets are awarded as learners improve their skills; obversely a green owl mascot turns up in your email if you don't appear regularly for your lesson. Some get as hooked on his omnipresence as a gamer might with Mario. Other users find the owl's surveillance creepy and I'm one of them. *À chacun son goût.*

   L As long as you're willing to take another look at an exercise our group did back in the day.

Let's say I could speak the French I yearn to *maîtriser*. Let me remind you of what it wouldn't look like by showing you some writing I did for our group in 2012:

*Julien <u>se fixe</u> sur la main de Mme de Rênal et on pourrait dire que les **rélations** sentimentales ressemblent à un **champs** de bataille. Quand il <u>s'annonce</u> qu' "il faut dire à cette femme que je l'aime" (p.64), c'est parce qu'il adopte la mentalité de son **idol** Napoléon. Saisir la main c'est aussi <u>prendre</u> le premier pas vers le soulagement de son âme et <u>terminer</u> "un affreux supplice" (p. 62) qui est jusqu'a présent l'histoire de sa vie. Comment effectuer cette action? Au lieu de se laisser aller vers des sentiments plus doux, Julien <u>calcule</u> <u>comme</u> il a **du** <u>faire pour subir</u> sa vie de jeune homme.*

You created the key below to help me correct my errors:

Corrigez les mots ou parties de phrases indiqués comme suit:

- *en **caractères gras**: erreur d'orthographe*

- *souligrés: erreur ou maladresse lexicale*

- *surlignés: erreur de structure*

I labored over this meager paragraph and it was discouraging to have made any errors at all with a dictionary at my disposal. The breathless moment in *Le rouge et le noir* when Julien finally dares to reach for Mme de Rênal's hand deserved better. My own overreactions aside, the key above tells the truth of the matter: I've got a long road ahead when it comes to writing French. Along the way there will be spelling errors, omissions, and vocabulary blunders galore. I'm not entirely sure what a *maladresse lexicale* is, by the way, and this is just for starters.

LE ROUGE ET LE NOIR

L Hired as a tutor by the prosperous mayor of a provincial village, Julien Sorel plans the conquest of his employer's wife as if he were conducting a military campaign in the style of his idol, Napoleon. The affair is eventually discovered and the ambitious young seducer from a peasant family is off to Paris, where he will wind up wooing the daughter of another employer, the Marquis de la Mole. Julien's passions are a shifting play of light and dark. Tracking his interior monologues is only one reason to read this curiously contemporary psychological novel published in 1830, just fifteen years after Napoleon's defeat at Waterloo.

C *Une maladresse lexicale* is a clumsy word choice: not incorrect but not idiomatic either — by no means a grammatical error, as is the case with most errors you and others make along the way. Some food for thought to start …

Now for a comment that was either missing — *en ce cas, mes plus plates excuses* — or forgotten: Your "meager paragraph" is no ordinary piece of writing, but a subtle, evocative analysis which, save a few glitches, flows rather well. My correction key brings attention — not judgment — to these glitches to help reflect on what went wrong and why. I can only repeat what many have said before, errors are necessary steps in the learning process, and ask you to welcome them. They will — and in fact should — be made, questioned, understood, corrected, and made again, and again, until one day *ce dont* or *desquelles* pops out at the right place and time in the midst of conversation. Till then, the clown in me may surprise the stumbler with a wink, a funny face, or even a fake heart attack, for after all, grammar rhymes with laughter, and so does error.

L   I've always suspected that theater — and being theatrical — is a huge part of successful teaching and learning. I wish mistakes didn't make me break out in hives.

C   I'll give this one last shot. Listen to what a student of mine recently said in class when discussing professional abilities: "*Pour être avocat, il faut être organisé parce que les avocats traiter beaucoup de documents.*" The use of the infinitive *traiter* instead of the conjugated form *traitent* seemed a conscious choice, not a mistake, so I asked about it. His answer was that the first two infinitives both expressed general ideas: "In order to be a lawyer, one must be organized." Since "handling documents" is as routine as "being organized" in the world of law, he decided not to conjugate the third verb either. I congratulated him on his faulty logic. It showed that errors can be organic, intelligible parts of the learning process.

L   Thanks for distinguishing between conscious choice and a mistake. Sometimes there actually is a reason a non-native speaker like me consistently pairs *si* with the conditional, for example. It takes a discerning teacher to do a grammar intervention by asking why.

C   Even more important is to know when to intervene. I let a number of errors fly by (in oral interaction) just because thorough corrections would defeat the purpose, which is to encourage flow. The mistakes systematically addressed in class are tied to the grammatical concepts that must be acquired — and solidly in place — in order for students to accomplish specific tasks. But more about "tasks" later.

L   Any examples of errors you would ignore?

C Off the top of my head no such examples, but a question I should have ignored. Skimming through a news article, some students pointed to a perplexing E at the end of *faite* in "*la proposition qu'il a faite.*" They had just learned and ached over the *passé composé* past participle agreement with *avoir* and *être* and here comes that E blowing a brand-new deal. Justifying its presence and logic required tools the beginners' class did not have and was not ready to even consider. But there was no going around the daunting vowel. So I explained. One heartfelt "Jesus!" detonated, echoed by a dozen laughing faces.

L It was a big moment when Renée admitted to being an *esclave de la grammaire.* For a learner to be enthralled and sometimes hobbled by the rigors and beauty of grammar is easy to understand. That mastery could be a form of oppression was a new one for me.

LES "SI" N'AIMENT PAS LES "RAIS"

L One of my favorite blunders is doubling up on the conditional when a sentence begins with *si.* The ending *rais* seems to go well with another *rais,* like wine and cheese. Except that it doesn't. A couple of *françaises* proved this by duking it out over this issue in an online chat room. The winner put it simply: "*les 'si' n'aiment pas les 'rais.*'"

The Bescherelle website is even more emphatic on this score. Not only does it reiterate the rule, it quotes Petit Gibus when he says, "*Ah ben mon vieux, si j'aurais su, j'aurais pas venu,*" in the film *La guerre des boutons.* The poor little guy is left *tout nu* after the neighboring village kids tear the buttons from his clothing. What seems to have made this scene famous, if the Internet response is any measure, is not his poignant exit as he turns to go. It's his misuse of the conditional.

C With this thought comes a memory, the time when I realized what subtle, unequivocal meaning *le mode subjonctif* conferred — a power that irrevocably altered my idea of grammar: no longer just a set of rules but a coherent system I longed to explore.

L I have a corresponding memory from our group at The Carlyle. I wonder what you make of it now. We were trying to understand one aspect of the subjunctive and your corporeal demonstration of space

THE POWER OF THE SUBJUNCTIVE

L There's plenty of drama to focus on in *De rouille et d'os*, a film with Marion Cotillard as an animal trainer who has lost both legs to a killer whale and her heart to Matthias Schoenaerts, who plays a street fighter and haphazard father to a young son.

In the movie's preview, you don't have to speak French to see that our man is in trouble. Slumped in a chair, his eyes darting left and right as Cotillard slams him for going off with another girl in front of her very eyes, he's guilty and he knows it.

"Ça te semble bien qu'on ait cette conversation? Que je te demande comment c'était avec la fille d'hier et que tu me répondes que c'était normal?"

"Tu veux que je dis quoi là?"

Cotillard's use of the subjunctive in this scene and Schoenaerts' *dis*, instead of *dise*, stand out to someone preoccupied with the rules of language. He has behaved like an animal and it will be up to Cotillard to train him in much more than grammar. Several sentences later, after a long look at the Mediterranean, she lays down the law with quiet strength.

"Si tu veux qu'on continue il faut faire les choses bien. Il faut qu'on ait des manières."

If they're going to be together, they'll have to treat each other with delicacy. He nods in silent acquiescence. Perhaps he's as subdued by the power of language as he is by his own misbehavior.

illustrated that beautifully. You cupped one hand in front of your body, as if holding a book.

"Using the subjunctive can indicate an appreciation of reality. One that requires an emotional distance between the observer and the observed," you explained, pulling back your other hand to further elongate that distance — and barely missing the sconce on the wall behind you. The physical demonstration reinforced the rule and made sense in a way that words alone often don't.

RECADRAGE

Les Chevaliers du Subjonctif

C *"Oh ... Il faut que j'y vais demain,"* interrupted Marguerite, suddenly reminding herself, in the midst of our conversation, of an appointment she had the following day. One of twelve children and, years later, the single working mother of four, Marguerite has juggled her share of doubts and fear and fought many battles in her life. She could have joined the ranks of *les chevaliers du subjonctif*, the knights from Erik Orsenna's novel, a bunch of freedom fighters bent on saving the mood — *"le dernier pays des rêves ... le lieu de tous les possibles,"* says critic Olivier Le Naire — from dictatorship and extinction. Only she didn't know it existed.

At eighty, she shared her life with Eugène, a close friend of ours, and on the day of our visit, the happy eighty-second-birthday boy. The rounds of Riesling toasts to his health were not to blame for her jarring mistake. Both she and Eugène grew up the children of working-class families in Sainte-Marie-aux-Mines, a small town in the heart of Alsace. Marguerite's blunder is a marker of social class, region, and time: it is often made by Alsatian workers born in the 1930s of parents who were German citizens.

What she and Matthias Schoenaerts happen to have in common is language upbringing. Although misidentified as French, the actor is Belgian of Flemish origin and a Dutch native speaker, in a country where French is spoken by half its people. That he missed — and probably ignores — a basic subjunctive structure in this scene is startling, no question, but his foreign background — both in real and fictitious life as Ali, his character's first name, may suggest — won the empathy of the FSL teacher and Alsatian in me. Linda is right, he "has behaved like an animal." Now does his grammar *faux pas* make him sound like one? Not to my ears, at least ... but to director Jacques Audiard's? Did he choose to ignore the actor's slip or was it actually part of the script? Whichever the case, he seems to think that subjunctive mishaps are as convincing as belly fat — which he insisted Schoenaerts put on for the role — to portray a working-class guy.

C *Je suis surprise — et heureuse — que tu t'en souviennes.*

By saying *"je suis surprise"* or *"heureuse,"* I voice my opinion about a fact (your remembering my physical demonstration). Taking a step back to

PEPÉ LE PEW

L How is it that I always opt for *je peut* instead of *je peux*? If I can say it so often and energetically, why can't I spell it? I could drop the whole thing and write the more literary *je puis*, but skirting the issue is no way to learn. When a cartoon character from my youth popped into my head, I wondered whether the character's name might serve as a mnemonic device and decided to follow where the stinky French skunk led me.

Created in 1945, Pepé Le Pew isn't the hapless suitor I remember. A lot of outraged people on YouTube see him as a stalker and worse, rather than a perpetually lovesick guy who is doomed to rejection because of his smell.

OK, so he does come on strong, too strong for some. And I don't like thinking about the effect his cartoons might have had on impressionable young minds in his heyday. But next time I conjugate *pouvoir* (or *vouloir* for that matter), thinking of Pepé Le Pew as Pepé *je peux/veux (appeler la police, te casser la figure)* may help me remember that X.

have a better look at us that Saturday at The Carlyle and reflect on your memory requires the subjunctive, although reality is neither questioned nor fantasized — roles the mood is best known for — but because subjectivity is involved.

What do I make of that physical demonstration now? I smile, and see how devoted I was to grammar. *La grammaire a du sens* had by then become my teaching motto and "Does each rule have a purpose?" a question that would never quite release its hold.

"Enthralled and sometimes hobbled." After all, your hang-up with grammar reflects the fear and lust experienced by many — teachers and masters included.

L Grammar can trigger powerful emotions. Tracing a little online etymology via Dictionary.com helps make sense of why: "In the Middle Ages gramarye was restricted to 'high' learning, written in Latin and including occult sciences and magic." That gramarye comes to us from the Old French *gramaire* is no surprise.

C Now that I think of it, *grimoires* — sorcerers' ritual handbooks — must be derived from the same root…Why such a spell? Common sense and intuition dictate my answer. As the standing operating procedures of language, grammar is to be learned and applied.

Other components — pronunciation, for instance, or the art of storytelling — require creativity, disposition, or talent that, one, study may never yield and two, are appraised differently depending on taste, culture, or education. Not everybody enjoys a Swiss accent or a speaking style *à la* François Busnel. The codes of grammar, on the other hand, can be cracked and reproduced either successfully or not. With the exception of spelling, that either-right-or-wrong quality applies to no other part of language. Slang is no less meaningful than standard vocabulary, dull ideas no less true than smart ones, foreign accents no less clear than native inflections. But "no less" does not apply to rules. With grammar, "correct" equals "perfect." A pairing that gives wings — or paralyzes.

L Paralysis and perfection can go hand in hand. There's no wiggle room with grammar, unless it's the wiggling we do when confronting the terminology that defines it. *Proposition subordonnée, compléments d'objet indirect* — my brain freezes as soon as I encounter those words. I once read of a movement in French schools to present grammar without the labels. Sounds appealing, but how would you teach without the technical terms? Explaining what they do before we learn what they're called might be a good place to start.

C Language teachers can't just grab moods and conjunctions the way chefs grab cooking utensils to teach others how to cook. Technical

SWATCH!

C My mnemonic trick (the one I remember, at least) was Swatch — kind of ironic for someone who never wore a watch in her life! But Swatch would pop into my head every time I'd get "what" and "which" wrong. What happened was that I would confuse the two, which is no surprise since no such difference exists in French. *Ce qui se passait, c'était que je confondais les deux, ce qui n'a rien d'étonnant puisqu'on ne fait pas la différence en français.*

So "which" or "what"? Swatch! "S" for *suivre* (follow) and "watch" for "what": my own quirky formula to remember to use "what" when the pronoun referred to an idea that followed in the sentence, not one that had just been mentioned. Not as wicked as your Pepé, Linda, but certainly as personal. And forget about *je puis*, definitely too *guindé*.

terms cannot be seen, felt, or heard unless colors, props, and sounds are used instead — a rare thing. "What they do" must therefore, indeed, be explained, and the terms themselves used with moderation — as should some of the words they refer to.

Since you've brought up magic, allow me one last detour to fairyland. Cinderella's glass slipper and her stepsisters' ungainly feet just popped into my mind. An impossible fit. The Grand Duke's hopeless look must cross my own face sometimes. Wanting to cram as much language as possible into one sentence — or class — is as common a misstep for learners as it is for teachers. For many, to shine means to put on a grammar show.

L   Part of me would love to be in the audience. I can't imagine knowing enough over-the-top grammar to put it to use.

C   I bet another part of you believes in "less is more." Over-the-top doesn't suit a casual setting, even for sharing great thoughts. In fact, it can be rather awkward — think evening gown at a barbecue. The perfect orchestration, where complexity coalesces with clarity, style, and content, requires more than high-end grammar.

L   So down with the gown?

C   Yes! Maybe this last homage to Renée will finally convince you. She is the perfect example of someone who's fluent in grammar, yet unable to flow in conversation — not much of a surprise considering her circumstances: brutal, illiterate parents and years as a closed-off *concierge* don't make you a social queen. That said, she shows that mastery — and love — of grammar isn't all there is to fluency.

L   My children's dad was casual about the rules of language during our early years in France, yet his communication skills were remarkable. He had a job to do and there was no time to conjugate in the beginning. Verbs tended to remain in the infinitive, but this didn't inhibit his message from coming through loud and clear with friends, colleagues, and employees. He succeeded in getting his ideas across *sans* fretting over details.

C   Part of his success lies in the differences between writing and speaking, two distinct language enterprises. Not that one is easier than the other, but I'd dare say that speaking is more forgiving. Some blunders magically dissolve with pronunciation: How, for instance, to distinguish between the endings *é, és, ée, ées, ez, er, ai, ais, ait, aient* when all are identical sounds? Confusion rarely looks good on paper but can sound charming or funny. And so can drawing a blank. A gesture or paraphrase will fill the gap. *Bref,* talkers put on a very different kind of show.

L   If I loosened up and told my inner grammarian to pipe down on the first draft, chances are I would enjoy writing more. I certainly do that in English.

C   To master grammar is admirable. To assess the place it has in relation to other language skills and to context, and to give it that place, is to become freer with language. Fairer expectations, *non*?

L   *Chapeau.* You've put grammar in its place, *une fois pour toutes.* ❦

In Other Words
Vrais ou faux amis?

CLAIRE: **Big white teeth and a wide-open mouth are the liveliest memories of my first Arabic teacher.** We sat on opposite sides of his small desk for a couple of weeks, during which I took the private classes required to join the beginners' course a month after its official start. I was in my third year of college, and a fresh language-learning experience was a must for students interested in a master's degree in FSL — enough of a reason to admit a latecomer to the class. Mr. Addas and I hunkered down in his office until I could read, write, hear, and produce the twenty-nine consonant sounds of the Arabic alphabet. Without his vigorous vocal demonstrations, some would have remained mysteries to me and to be able to utter *qaf*'s and *ayn*'s is, to this day, my proudest phonetic achievement.

I wish our sonorous get-togethers had continued but once I joined my seventy or so classmates, courses were held in an amphitheater. Mr. Addas directed the ship from afar, reciting from *L'arabe langue vivante* behind a lecture stand. The textbook, published in the early '80s, offered the same series of activities page after page — a written dialogue followed by detailed grammar explanations, vocabulary lists, and translation exercises — and each chapter took us deeper into the Arabic ocean of rules.

The course suited my analytical nature. The exposure to a new way of thinking about language was enjoyable, in fact so much so as to dismiss reality for an entire year. But the only thing alive about *L'arabe langue vivante* was the word in the title. I was learning Arabic

VOCABULARY: WHAT SAYS THE CEFR?

C The twenty-six tasks of the French language program at the UN have been designed to cover the range of vocabulary expected at the B1 level of the CEFR in three hundred hours of class instruction: "Sufficient vocabulary [for a student] to express him/herself with some circumlocutions on most topics pertinent to his/her everyday life such as family, hobbies and interests, work, travel and current events."

Now, how much does "sufficient" add up to? The amount is proportionate to capacity, skill, and incentive to learn. What students must acquire is a "survival kit" to communicate in the plainest — yet intelligible — way.

The Common European Framework of Reference for Languages was born in the early '90s, when, in welcoming new members, the European Union faced a sizable challenge: How to sustain cultural and linguistic diversity in a world dominated by English? The answer — encouraging Europeans to speak one another's languages and travel, study, or live abroad — required consistency in language learning, teaching, and assessment across countries. By achieving this, the CEFR has become a standard for describing language ability both in Europe and internationally.

The CEFR's six broad levels range from A1 or breakthrough level — described on the DELF-DALF website as "the point at which the learner can interact in a simple way, ask and answer simple questions about themselves, initiate and respond to simple statements in areas of immediate need or on very familiar topics" — to C2 which, although "it has been termed 'mastery' is not meant to imply native-speaker or near native-speaker ability," but characterizes a high "degree of precision, appropriateness and ease with the language."

the same way as I had been studying ancient Greek, except Nadir and Zaynab had taken the place of gods and emperors. The textbook characters, whom I did not once hear, were black-and-white cartoon figures sketched next to dialogue boxes. Language learning turned into a purely intellectual enterprise, which I'd have agreed to pursue had I been able to interact outside the classroom.

Only I was not. The first words I read in Arabic included "grasshopper," "rope," "sailboat," "alarm clock," "fishing net," and on went the list of useless terms for a student eager to greet people and introduce herself. Vocabulary merely served phonetic and grammatical purposes. As a result, sentences had been put together regardless of their relevance or likeliness to be reproduced. Who, but a dull poet, would ever say, "On the gardener's dog's head is a small green leaf" (lesson 8) or "I am planing a long plank" (lesson 12)? After a year of study, I was still missing some key words to have a basic conversation: Without "French," "student," "university," "twenty-two years old," I was bound to cut myself short. Too short to keep up with even cartoon friends.

L   *Mabrouk* (congratulations) for surviving that frustrating year. How much time does it take your students to learn how to navigate a basic exchange in French?

C   What would that exchange be about and where and with whom would it take place? Buying a *croissant* in a *boulangerie* takes fewer and different words than booking a hotel room on the phone. Context and purpose are central to language (and more so vocabulary) instruction: they determine which words are relevant to "navigate an exchange."

What would your tool kit, my own fancy term for them, hold if, for example, you had to apply for a visa in a French consulate? Words asking you to spell your first and last names, indicate your nationality, age, marital status, profession, address, and phone number, and words to greet, thank, provide the requested information, or say you don't understand. Twenty hours of class is about right for UN French 1 students to assemble their visa application tool kit — before they put it to use.

How about you, Linda? How much time did it take to strike up a conversation with the Saint-Paulois?

L   Invitations to sample our neighbor's paella began to roll in as soon as we moved there and so did the opportunities for informal learning. Other social opportunities surfaced, some more successful than others. I picked nervously at my food during a luncheon, thrilled and terrified to be included in the small gathering. I could barely follow the conversation between old friends, let alone contribute to the exchange. When my host noted that I must not have liked my salad, I replied that it was *très riche*, producing gales of laughter and a lively discussion of American salads. I didn't know how to explain that the salad was filling — and that I was *un paquet de nerfs*.

My vocabulary in France developed within a strict context — raising children and creating a home in another country. I'm not sure that made me as deliberate as your students at the UN, but I knew I needed words in this new world, words of every ilk.

When my son was born, my midwife folded her arms over her chest and asked me whether he was *sage*. How could a newborn be well-

LOST AND FOUND

L   Once we returned to the States, my daughter's American vocabulary owed much to the books she burned through during her final two years in France. Informed by the vernacular in the *Sweet Valley High* series, she adopted the speech patterns of the teens featured in those books. A fierce reader in English and in French, when she wasn't in Sweet Valley mode her discourse mirrored whatever she was reading at the time. My son had a French-only policy in France. Our return meant he would have to make his way through fourth grade in the very English he had shunned. But by the end of that trying year, he had successfully graduated from strictly French to strictly English. Their issues with language and vocabulary were normal, as they had been enrolled almost exclusively in French schools, but what was the deal with their mom?

For a long time after our return, my English syntax was way off. Worse, there seemed to be a dybbuk inside my brain bent on stealing the exact word I needed when no other word would do. A different form of this Lost Word Syndrome has resurfaced since, only this time the lost word is usually French. If an approximate word pops into my head that I'm not sure works, I give it a shot anyway when in the company of French speakers, whom I can count on to correct me. At other times I may simply tire of my familiar vocab and try to strike out in new directions. I recently tried *narrer* instead of *raconter*. Saying it felt unfamiliar and a little awkward, but it got me where I wanted to go. I had more luck with that than *mariner*, another word that was technically correct, but that went nowhere in a real conversation.

behaved, I wondered, and did crying disqualify him? Even more puzzling was the fact that the midwife was called a *sage-femme*. It was a word I would hear repeatedly as my kids made their way through the French school system, but not once did it mean wise. *Sois sage*, mothers would remind their children as they dropped them off for the day. The admonishment was as standard as the kiss they received before the moms hurried off to work.

I picked up plenty of words from my own children, *berk* being a prime example. Both kids struggled with lunchtime *à la cantine*. My daughter detested *semoule*, a mixture of cheese and durum wheat she hid inside her napkin. *Prout*, slang for fart, was accompanied by sound effects that produced giggles in the backseat of the car. My vocabulary expanded without maturing as I absorbed what my children brought back from school, but I didn't care. I got a kick out of saying *fastoche* instead of *facile*.

There was nothing *fastoche* about the night we rushed our toddler son to the hospital in Nice. We were in too much of a hurry to call our English-speaking village doctor. Christopher's breathing was labored and he couldn't stop rubbing his bleary eyes and red nose. How did you say "asthma" in French and did that have anything to do with the eczema that tortured him? *Piqûres. Ampoules. Crise de foie.* My medical vocabulary was limited to what I'd picked up reading labels in our local pharmacy or listening to reports from friends on the effects of eating too much good food. The pantomime that ensued at the hospital ended almost as soon as it began. "*Voilà, petit bonhomme.*" The *haricot vert* was extracted from my son's nose, and we laughed weakly over the exploits of a very active toddler and picky eater. I'm not sure what words I added to my tool kit that night, but my son survived and so did I.

C What you experienced in France is context-based learning at its best and very much what teachers strive to recreate in class: a situation where students have no choice but to make use of specific words — like your *maman* tool kit — in order to learn them.

L Life would have been very different if I'd had an iPhone back in the day. Then again, would I have really been present during those crazy early interactions with my head bent over a cell phone?

C *Pas sûr.* The battle against smartphones in the classroom has been my longest to date. I thought about adding "and no translation" to the "no food or drinks allowed" sign to substantiate my plea for a dictionary-free zone. "What's wrong with looking up words we don't know?" is the question never asked. I would answer by flagging the danger of decontextualized words in bilingual dictionaries, where making the right choice is all but chance. What, for example, does "step" mean in the sentence, "Our next step should be to ban Google Translate": *pas, marche, ou étape?*

L I would probably go with *pas.*

C Nope. *La prochaine étape serait d'interdire Google Translate.* Yours is a common *faux pas,* pun intended, but things can get worse, even in the highest circles. Claude Piron, famous for his works in and about Esperanto and former translator at the United Nations, wrote: "Think of the plight of Danish Minister Helle Degn who meant to say, at the outset of an international meeting, that she had just taken up her functions and said: 'I'm at the beginning of my period.'"

L I feel her pain. I might have reached for the word *fonctions* had it been in my survival kit, if only because it looks like "functions."

BEST TOOL KIT EVER

C *Une épicerie* is not your average deli, especially when it is *fine,* and *l'Arabe du coin* not a great thing to say — or ask for. So no French word for "deli"?

Si. The Québécois found one.

And they didn't stop at food: with them, *dépannage* took another dimension. If unsure about grammar, or spelling, or vocabulary, or punctuation, or pronunciation, or … — yes, the list goes on — la Banque de dépannage linguistique has the answer. We're not talking deli here; la BDL is the *épicerie fine* for language lovers. Definitely worth a visit.

Not sure that word does the job, but it would have spared the Danish minister some embarrassment.

C It does — and offers the perfect segue into my next point: what an invaluable resource English can be. The tendency to warn against false cognates (words that look alike but have different meanings) eclipses the thousands of *vrais amis* French and English have in common. Abandon, abdication, abdomen, aberration, abolition, abominable, just these first few are enough to see how wide and rich our shared vocabulary is.

L Are these your true friends, too? I think of the transactions between French and English you must make on a daily basis.

LEAVING ROOM

L Sometimes mistakes pay off. American poet Catherine Barnett thought duration (English) should be *la duration* (French). And can you blame her? Things got even more complicated when her friends heard *l'adoration* instead. She makes the most of the confusion in her poem "Essay on 'An Essay Concerning Human Understanding.'" Would Barnett have taken her roundabout journey — or written this particular poem — without making the gaffe? Coming across her work torn from the pages of the *New Yorker* and buried under papers on my desk was a reminder to tidy my workspace, reflect on some mistakes of my own, and to always, always leave room for poetry.

C Yes, and also best friends! They allow me to teach almost entirely in French even at the beginner level. For example, "*La voyelle E en position finale est muette*" is a sentence that English-speaking students new to the language can understand provided they phonetically "bridge" words they hear for the first time and words they know.

L Not sure I'd instantly make the leap from *muette* to "mute." Two syllables versus one would throw me off. I might also get sidetracked by the fact that *muette* rhymes with *pirouette* and *cacahuète*, remnants from a children's song that were part of my *maman* tool kit. All kinds of associations kick in when I'm grappling with an unfamiliar word. Am I a party of one?

RHYMING O'S

C   Who knew that "*métro, boulot, dodo,*" the French epitome of city life, originally appeared in a poem? I didn't, nor had I heard of its author, Pierre Béarn (born Louis-Gabriel Besnard), *homme de lettres français* little known by *le grand public* despite a prolific career and remarkable life.

Au déboulé garçon
pointe ton numéro

Pour gagner ainsi le salaire

D'un morne jour utilitaire

Métro, boulot, bistro,
mégots, dodo, zéro

The last lines of "Synthèse," published in the collection *Couleurs d'usine* (1951), paints the life of an orphaned child compelled to work for subsistence, which Béarn himself experienced at age fourteen. In May 1968, two thousand copies of the poem were printed and circulated among the unruly Parisian students, and before long "*métro, boulot, dodo*" covered the walls of the Sorbonne. Summing up the drudgery and routine of the worker's life, the three words — *métro* refers to the subway commute, *boulot* is *argot* for "work" or "job," and *dodo* baby talk for "sleep" — quickly became the rallying cry of *les ouvriers* who joined the protests.

Still in fashion *en France et ailleurs*, *le slogan soixante-huitard* has inspired a few others, mostly devised by and for women — "*marmots, boulot, dodo*" is one of them. Like the working mums, union members in recent protests against a hike in the retirement age kept close to the original three words.

But I say we get bolder. Aristocrats? "*Château, polo, Clicquot.*" Partygoers? "*Resto, disco, pavot.*" Intellectuals? "*Expo, dico, info.*" And who could "*rando, bistrot, philo*" be about? My kind of people, *les amateurs de marches et de bonne chair — des philosophes sans le savoir.*

C   You're not, and I was just about to distinguish "easy" leaps, made possible with true cognates, from others, requiring more craft and confidence. Linking *muette* to "mute," as you pointed out, or *voyelle* to "vowel" isn't as obvious as leaping from *position* to "position," although even this one proves a challenge for students unaccustomed to new sounds — in which case I resort to writing. That pretty much does the trick and puts big smiles on puzzled faces.

Mais revenons aux ami(e)s. Have you and your *Larousse* become true friends? And how do you keep amassing words now that French neighbors and dinners are no more?

L   With spoken language no longer as available as it once was, I've turned primarily to the written word, with varying results. French words that roll off the tongue of a lavish speaker or nestle inside sentences on

LIVING LANGUAGE DAILY CALENDAR

L   The most appealing way I've found to keep forging on in French is to read books. In the spirit of experiment, I recently bought a pack of *crayons-feutres* to brighten up my marginalia. Maybe color-coding underlined words and their definitions will help my retention.

There are plenty of ways to keep up with new words or structures. One of my favorites is the Living Language Daily Phrase and Culture Calendar. A sentence a day, when judiciously composed, can be a powerful learning tool. *"Cela s'annonce comme un véritable défi"* got my attention one October. What did I get out of this seemingly simple sentence? A non-nagging reminder that *défi* is a challenge it's best not to defy. Maybe I'll even try *cela s'annonce* rather than the *ça* that comes more naturally.

When I'm finished with my page, I flip it over to create a grocery list (*en français* if I'm feeling energetic). Instead of bolting down the aisle at the market, I amble and browse the labels. Much is marked in French as well as English and it's a shame not to notice. The content from the back of a box isn't a great conversation starter, but it refreshes what I already know and often throws some new ingredients into the mix. *Faites gaffe* if you try to photograph the coffee grinder in your local Trader Joe's, however: taking a photo of the hinged metal flap that is also a *rabat* may produce a different sort of flap with personnel.

a page are an invitation to discovery. I'm using *Le Petit Larousse*, an illustrated dictionary intended for the whole family. A picture here and there makes the hefty volume easier to approach.

WINE VOCAB

C Did you know a bottle alone could boost your French? And before you even drink it! Brand names are changing for the better — at least in the French section of my local *caviste* in Brooklyn. Forget about castles and Gothic fonts: the new generation of wine labels pique curiosity and inform. "*Du premier coup d'œil, le consommateur doit savoir ce qu'il peut attendre du vin qu'il va déguster*," writes Marie Lecrosnier-Wittkowsky in her article "Tout savoir sur les étiquettes de vin et leur sens!"

See for yourself. One good look at this label — *et de la suite dans les idées* — will solve the mystery of Saint Glinglin, both the idiom and the wine.

"Awesome Bordeaux every day," says the back label, "meant to be drunk and enjoyed, not traded and hoarded. We're intent on putting it back on your table. Every day." The day when pigs fly, la Saint Glinglin, has finally come. So has a miracle wine.

Now look at these. No visual clues this time, but creative, clever, and fitting names that should tickle your taste buds — and pairing skills. Not pairing wines with food, but with adjectives I've chosen just for you.

So you've got *trois noms* — Cent Visages, L'Hurluberlu, Les Impénitents — and now *trois adjectifs*: opulent, versatile, original. Which wine is which? *Vous hésitez?* Throw a tasting party. And taste generously, for it will take more than one glass of L'Hurluberlu to say it right. *Santé!*

THE SPACE BETWEEN WORDS

L *The Lacemaker*, the movie based on *La dentellière*, launched Isabelle Huppert's career. Its translation to film couldn't have been simple. How to dramatize the interior life of Pomme, a shampoo girl in a hair salon so named because of her shiny, apple-red cheeks, when silence is her principal form of communication? Her suitor and eventual detractor Aimery is a university student from a comfortable family. He courts her until he becomes increasingly frustrated with her passivity, then leaves her abruptly. The sudden shift in narration from third person to first at the end of the book is as provocative as author Pascal Lainé must have intended it to be. The intricacies of language explored in the prose suggest the lace in the title. No wonder I wanted to capture every word in this 1974 Goncourt Prize–winning novel.

Lately it's less about *Le petit Larousse* than it is about technology. I know you discourage running to the dictionary each and every time I feel the need to know, but some of us have trouble with impulse control. When reading French on my iPhone, I hold my finger on a word I don't recognize for a second and let the screen take me to the Web for a quick and easy definition. I know, I know. Momentary gratification isn't the same as genuine vocabulary building, an expression I've heard you use. If dreams ever did come true, there would be a way for that word to be instantly — and forever — absorbed by the same simple touch.

C *À jamais* does raise the bar, even higher for solo learners. The back-and-forth triggered by *un mot nouveau* cements it in memory. How, then, to build and retain meaning without classmates and instructors to discuss words with? Any *trucs* you'd be willing to share?

L Tricks? No. But I have plenty of habits that mean secondhand booksellers aren't likely to be beating a path to my door.

As I flip through books I've loved or merely endured, one thing stands out: they are all respectfully defaced. Some words are underlined with two bold strokes, signaling that I've been down that road more than once. Illegible synonyms are occasionally scribbled in the margins. *La dentellière*, by Pascal Lainé, is hysterically underscored with definitions for unfamiliar words squeezed into every available corner and *s'évertuer* is one of them. I was striving all right, both to get inside the narrator's mind and enrich my own vocabulary by borrowing from his.

But not every word captures my imagination in the same way — they often wind up noted, but unclaimed. These underlined word orphans need a home. My plan for most books, though not always executed, is to finish and return after I'm done to look up marginal terms I didn't recognize. As a writer, I struggle to find *le mot juste*, so it pains me to label any word marginal. But sometimes I'm too engrossed in the narrative to stop, unless they are words that truly bring my understanding of the story to a halt. Knowing that a *bouvreuil* is a bullfinch didn't actually enhance my first read of *Les âmes grises*, a novel by Philippe Claudel. In practical terms, knowing what that word means is about as helpful as your Arabic grasshopper.

C Yes and no. Yes, because *bouvreuils* and *janaadib* make rare appearances in standard conversation. And no, because your *bouvreuil* was part of a story you chose and felt compelled to read. My *jundub* hopped from nowhere into a grammar exercise. Neither words have remained with us, but your encounter was organic whereas mine was forced. I am convinced that crossing paths with words in real situations (novels, movies, phone calls, meetings, etc.) is the first step towards finding them a home.

L And claiming ownership. What to do with all those underlined words I have studiously looked up is a conundrum. On zealous days,

---

LES ÂMES GRISES

L The prize-winning novel *Les âmes grises* is an account of the twenty-year-old murder case of young Belle-de-Jour by an aging policeman who worked the case years before. The policeman's interiority, the period language of 1917, and the Great War exploding in the near distance make for a rigorous vocabulary exercise, but it's worth it. Philippe Claudel was lured away from punk rock into writing and teaching and is never without his grandfather's pocket knife, though these days he uses literature *pour ouvrir le cœur*. What's not to love?

SPECIAL FIRSTS

C Special and personal: *ces premières fois* take place in my psychoanalyst's office — when I catch an English word I've never used before crossing my lips.

"What does that word mean, Dr. P?"

"What do you think it means?"

Every so often these newcomers create the unexpected. To think that words *dont j'ignore le sens* actually help me understand myself is, *si je puis dire*, mind-blowing.

my goal is retention, but how to accomplish that when the occasions for use are few and far between? French definitions in the margins rather than English is a technique I try in fits and starts. It's fun to know that the *geignard* in *Les âmes grises* is also a *pleurnichard*. Both of them are whiners, but will I retain either one? There's a good chance I might, if I think hard enough about the "*ard*"endings of both and a fresh connection I made not long ago between *se débrouiller* and *débrouillard*, a term I heard for the first time that means resourceful.

C I remember my fascination at the discovery of one magical tie woven into the fabric of history, a two-way bridge between English and French, vocabulary and conjugation: The verbs *abolir, accomplir, banir, chérir, démolir, garnir, établir, fleurir, polir, ravir,* and a dozen more not only all have English equivalents ending in -ish (abolish, accomplish, banish, etc.) but also happen to all be regular -ir verbs. No exception to the rule.

L *Sans blague?*

C No kidding. A French verb ending in *-ir* is regular provided it has an English "twin" ending in -ish. *Embellir?* Regular! *Acquérir?* Irregular! What invasions, royal love affairs, and trade deals coalesced to form such a unique bond? I wonder.

Another stirring vocabulary experience took place shortly after I returned to Arabic classes (and to an experience very different from my college years). The Al Jazeera journalist covering the death of Yasser Arafat kept on saying "*al-sheikh mat,*" "the king is dead." "Think of chess," said our teacher to help us understand. "Checkmate!" The answer swept across the room, and with it, astonishment at the fact that the Arabic phrase existed in each of our languages — French (*échec et mat*), German (*schachmatt*), Italian (*scacco matto*), Spanish (*jaque mate*), even Japanese (*chekkumeito*) and Polish (*szach mat*).

Vocabulary "moments" are among my favorites whether I am teaching or taking a class, mainly because they are not planned. An observation, a question, and the class zooms out from a sentence to a bigger picture. Those travels through languages and cultures are not only rewarding, they ease — and reconcile — the daunting memorization of words.

ACCROS À LACLOS

C *"Quand, après m'être creusé la tête pendant des heures et des jours, je trouvais les solutions à 'Collectionneur de papillons' ou 'Toujours en tête à la mairie' ... j'étais tout simplement heureux."*

Gérard Jugnot's homage to the *Nobel des mots croisés* says it all, and well. Happy, indeed, is any crossword puzzle enthusiast who gets to play with — and against — Michel Laclos. For "*des heures et des jours*" is how long it can take to see what *l'empereur des formules* gives us to look at: rarely the obvious. *Collectionneur de papillons?* Ditch the butterfly net, look past the flower fields, think hard — and don't stop before you've remembered (or learned) that *papillon* is also slang for parking ticket. Oooh ...

Never before did you think of *essuie-glaces* as butterfly collectors, did you? That's when happiness kicks in — and that first time is addictive.

L Daunting is an understatement. How would I consciously memorize words anyway? Write them again and again or sing them to myself in the car? Maybe I could listen to them in my sleep, as several websites suggest, to wake up a more eloquent me.

L'EAU EST BONNE

L I just unearthed a transcription that Claire made for our book group of an interview by Bernard Pivot of English-born Jane Birkin. The singer/actress was formerly married to singer Serge Gainsbourg and, although I find her perfectly fluent, some of her language struggles were similar to ours. Gainsbourg was surely putting her on when he assured her that anything with legs was feminine. Too bad she didn't join us the day Margot shared a *truc* that has stuck with me ever since.

She came up with a way of remembering the gender of water when one of her Belgian cousins announced that "*l'eau est bonne.*" Take a noun, any noun, then pair it with an adjective easy or outlandish enough to remember and you're on your way to maneuvering the gender minefield. Recently the he vs. she debate has become politicized, with battle lines drawn between teachers promoting gender-inclusive instruction and hard-liners like L'Académie française.

With so many questions left unanswered, I cave, and just do what transforms work into play. Cross-referencing words and characters, characters and authors is a pastime that can, with luck, lead to one of your vocabulary "moments." Sometimes all the activity can get pretty circuitous.

I once wondered whether the Guerlante, a fictional river in *Les âmes grises*, had anything to do with Guermantes Way, a route through memory and countryside in Proust's *In Search of Lost Time*. A quick Google search didn't reveal the connection I was after, but the detour through Jean-Baptiste Harang's review of *Les âmes grises* in *Libération* was worth the diversion:

Justement, l'hiver 1917, sur les bords d'une rivière minuscule, la Guerlante (aussi lente que l'autre, de guerre lasse, qui s'enlise et enlise avec elle tout l'humain), on découvre le corps, intact et mort, d'une toute jeune enfant, splendide petite princesse "aux lèvres bleuies et aux paupières blanches."

The sober play on words (Guerlante = *la guerre lente*) led me to another term I didn't know: *guerre lasse.* So that's what the lassitude after a long period of resistance is called. Not only that, but L'internaute, my favorite website for quick definitions, states that *guerre lasse* translates as "for the sake of peace and quiet," something we all need from time to time.

I didn't think I would wind up there, but it turns out pleasure can have a practical payoff. All those arrows and exclamation marks, obscure references to books that have no obvious connection to the one with all the scribbling, occasionally stick to the slippery surface of my mind. For that I am grateful and glad. ❧

Now You're Talking
Une affaire de rythme

LINDA: In 2012 my inveterate New Yorker husband and I pulled up stakes for Los Angeles. Leaving the French group was a tough goodbye and underscored the fact that I would be even farther from France. How was I going to keep my connection to the language — and the country — alive? Feasting on memories only went so far, especially as many of them had already begun to fade.

Here's one, though, that has remained vivid to this day. After our group met at The Carlyle, you and I sometimes headed south through Central Park to take the subway to Union Square. The walks were often as fruitful as the hours we'd spent at the hotel. To review a discussion while it was still warm was exactly what I needed to grapple with subordinate conjunctions, cause and consequence being my special bugaboo, until the next time I forgot whether *si bien que* was one or the other. One afternoon we stopped to watch a sparrow peck at a piece of bread until a blue jay muscled him out of the picture. I asked you to repeat your story of the child, the bird, and "the zone of confusion," a term I love and embrace to this day.

"When grown-ups say *un oiseau*, a child may hear *un noiseau*. Same thing goes for a squirrel."

That *un écureuil* could become *un nécureuil* seemed a wonderful thing to know. Blue sky and blustery wind, four friends as nutty for French as I was, and The Carlyle — my good luck was too much.

"*Je suis si contente*," I said, grabbing your arm for good measure.

"Linda, that is so French!"

Huh? To think that inadvertently slurring two single syllable words and binding them together to create *chui* was not only OK, but more French than keeping them separate but equal, was an eye-opener. What other language tics had I unconsciously picked up along the way and were they more useful than I knew?

C Were I a bolder teacher, or one with more faith in her students' sense of humor, I'd show them "The Offensive Translator," an episode of *The Catherine Tate Show*, the popular — and very British — sketch comedy series. Catherine Tate plays Helen Marsh, a woman who claims "I can do that!" in response to anything friends or colleagues need. Interpreting — not translating, the title is in error — English into seven languages at a big finance meeting? Yes she can! As clichéd as it is, her improvised tour of world accents has pedagogical value. It shows us how universal representations of languages are. Head bobbing, bouncy B's and D's? Indian! Tongue stuck between the teeth, whistling S's? Spanish! Dancing hands and rolling R's? Italian! Huffs and puffs, fidgety lips? *Heu* … French. *Français, vraiment?* Helen Marsh captures the busy French mouth but sounds like a karateka practicing

BABY TALK

L Claire, you're in impressive literary company when it comes to noting elisions. One of my favorite Proustian *feuilles d'artichaut* appears in *À l'ombre des jeunes filles en fleurs*. Swann, now married to the once wanton Odette, grills their daughter upon coming home to a swarm of visitors. Who on earth is Mme Swann hosting now, he wants to know.

"'J'sais que son mari est employé dans un ministère, mais j'sais pas au juste comme quoi,' disait Gilberte en faisant l'enfant."

Swann corrects a daughter he clearly adores.

"'Comment, petite sotte, tu parles comme si tu avais deux ans.'"

In an earlier passage, the narrator scrutinizes the Swann family's lightest exchange, down to the missing liaison:

"'Comment allez-vous?' (qu'ils prononçaient tous deux 'commen allez-vous' sans faire la liaison du t, liaison, qu'on pense bien qu'une fois rentré à la maison je me faisais un incessant et voluptueux exercice de supprimer)."

her kick. She's missing the "pretty" or "soft" part, something often heard about French pronunciation, and the "pshh pshh pshh" sound — that *chui* you totally soaked up. Thank you for bringing it up by the way. It's the perfect opening for this chapter.

L   Catherine Tate couldn't be less PC. She does a great job of insulting everyone with her extemporaneous *tour du monde.* As I was running errands today I did my version of Marsh speaking English with a French accent. My untested theory is that this can be useful nonsense, although you wouldn't want an audience. Being stuck in LA traffic has its advantages.

C   I'm curious. What did Hélène teach you?

L   The first thing is impeccable posture, strangely enough. And the kind of taut speaking that goes with it, as if you were in a debate. I envision straight lines and angles, in contrast to that slithery *chui,* were it possible to sketch a sound. I'm not suggesting the French all stand up straight, but sometimes the language feels like it does. I hope you're not asking me to be consistent in this chapter.

C   Not if inconsistency means great images. Before looking at the "straight lines and angles," let's listen to that "slithery *chui*" again, a centerpiece of French pronunciation and rhythm.

L   Your turn to draw a picture.

C   I see a smooth road winding among the hills and hear the rustling sound of rain tapping the earth.

L   I like the rusticity. Could you say a bit more?

C   French words, unlike English ones, have no stressed syllables. All are pronounced with the same intensity (the smooth road) except for the final syllables (the hills) of rhythmic groups.

Now buckle up. The drive is a long one and may not be as smooth as the road. *C'est parti!* English words carry at least one stressed

GAD'S GOT RHYTHM

L   Moroccan-born French comic Gad Elmaleh is an equal opportunity stand-up. His one-hour performance in Montreal called *Gad Gone Wild* skewers Parisians, Moroccans, and Indians, but he has a special place in his heart for Americans. Whether it's our relaxed attitude about English grammar or our limited knowledge of other countries (*surtout le Maroc*), nothing gets past this guy. Is he a comic or a contortionist? Both. Watching him move through his routine is a spectacle in itself.

English-speaking learners struggling with the concept of French rhythmic groups should take a cue from Gad and turn things inside out for a minute. Imagine how a French speaker might feel who's anxious to stress the proper syllable in English. "Is it 'EM-phasis' or 'em-PHA-sis' or 'empha-SIS'?"

Gad asks an excellent question and here's another one: How did I miss his Facebook post promising a "gluten-free, dairy-free, duty-free" performance at the Wilshire Ebell in LA? Guess who just acquired a new follower on Twitter.

syllable. Example: The French **sound**scape is unusually me**lo**dious. The same sentence pronounced by a French speaker would sound like this: The French sound**scape** is unusually melo**dious**. No surprise, just a "rhythmic transfer" from French to English. Remember, our stressed syllables (the hills) are the very last of specific word groups (stretches of the smooth road). What goes on inside these groups is the pitter-patter of rain — the "pshh pshh pshh" sound. How is the drive so far?

L   Scenic. This helps me visualize that soundscape along with hearing it. Can you please tell me how to form these groups?

C   A rhythmic group is a sequence of words connected by meaning — and spoken in a single breath. One group, one idea, one breath. Yes? So tell me, how many groups in this sentence? *Avoir un cœur d'artichaut signifie tomber amoureux facilement et souvent.*

J'PEUX PAS, J'AI PISCINE

L In the midst of a text messaging fest with my daughter, I accidentally hit a button on my iPhone and a nice surprise appeared on the screen: *Madame Figaro* had apparently launched its first collection of *stickers inédits* to go with its app and I was one of the lucky recipients. The icons appeared above the keyboard in my messages app, not that I'd been paying particular attention.

J'peux pas I got, given our discussion about *chpeupa*. But what about *j'ai piscine*? Did that mean I have a pool or that I'm swimming in it? The answer could be both, if the YouTube video called "J'ai piscine," by Kevin Bonnet, aka Keen' V, is any measure.

According to the lyrics, the French ragga musician from Rouen *ne peut pas* have lunch with his mom, respond to the requests of hangers-on, or do much of anything but goof around in the pool with his *potes*. How much do I love my iPhone? Let me count the ways.

L Three?

C Right. Which ones?

L *Avoir un coeur d'artichaut. Signifie tomber amoureux. Facilement et souvent.*

C And in this one? *Edith Piaf roule les R's quand elle chante, pas quand elle parle.*

L Two. Only because I'm out of breath by the time I get to the comma.

C *À bout de souffle?* Great for movies, not for pronunciation. Try three: *Edith Piaf roule les R's. Quand elle chante. Pas quand elle parle.*

L Got it, though I'm still not clear on that "pshh pshh pshh" business.

C "One group, one idea, one breath" is missing a part — the critical part: one phonetic word. *Avoir un cœur d'artichaut,* five written words, is pronounced *avoiruncœurdartichau,* as if the words were tied together. Say it please.

L *Avoiruncœurdartichau.*

C Again, a tad faster. Hear the rain?

L I do. Let's try one more.

C *Quand elle chante, pas quand elle parle: quantèlchant, paquantèlparl.* Steady rainfall — and a close letter-to-sound correspondence. But this isn't a rule, not by a long shot. Forget about seeing, let alone understanding, *il n'y a plus de café, tu en refais?* the first (dozen) time(s) you hear *yaputcafé, tenrefai?* And the picture gets blurrier still when *chui, chaipa, chpeupa* etc. — well-known members of the French Slithery gang — start rolling in and out.

L I like the versatility of *chpeupa*. It can cover a lot of emotional ground (sleepless nights, cakes that don't rise, you name it) that *je ne peux pas* with its discrete syllables doesn't. My daughter and I have heard this so many times from French friends that it now appears in our text messages and has even acquired a hashtag. If one of us really wants to lay it on thick, we might say *chpeupa chui fatiguée* as a greeting instead of hello. The expression almost always helps us lighten up.

C My take on it won't be as fun. I recently read about "phonetic erosion," defined as "gradual shifts in language that play out over years of use." According to the author of the term, it is what caused "want to" to shrink to "wanna," for instance. The concept is plausible, certainly evocative, but I'd rather think of *chpeupa* and its consorts as the results of communion, not erosion. Letters disappear or turn into weird sounds because they're part of — squeezed into — the same rhythmic group. Kind of like the hug you exchange with a close friend.

L I'll take communion over erosion any day. What I'd like to know is how and why those sounds change.

C Let's examine *chaipa*. Step one, *ne* disappears (*je sais pas*) — as it always does *à l'oral*. Step two, E melts away (*j'sais pas*) — not unusual either. Step three involves high-end phonetics, so I'll sum it up briefly: J, flirting with S, morphs into "ch" (*ch'sais pas*) which promptly seduces its new neighbor (*chaipa*).

L What a nice spin on the sound of my favorite romance language. If only all phonetics were described this cleverly.

C Thanks, but you can forget about all this. You've got the French beat — and speaking in "discrete syllables" doesn't mean you are less skilled, or sound less cool. *Jenesaipa* vs. *chaipa*? Sprinkle vs. downpour. The only difference is how fast they will get your feet wet.

Do you remember when you picked up on the rhythm, or did you just have it *dans la peau* from the start?

L You're assuming a consciousness I don't have, but I'll take the compliment anyway. I tend to inadvertently pick up speech patterns from friends and family, whether I like it or not. Could we say that absorbing rhythmic groups is a key to French pronunciation?

C Absolutely. At least as important as producing clear, isolated sounds. Bring up French pronunciation in a conversation and R's, U's, maybe nasal vowels — sounds foreign to American ears — will be discussed. Rhythm? Never, in my experience. It is however the distinct "packaging of words" that makes understanding spoken French challenging, not the R's and U's. I slow down, speak in discrete syllables, even choose different words when my interlocutors can't absorb rhythmic groups. And I too will be confused if they pause where they shouldn't, more so than if they mispronounce.

L Your last statement comes as a surprise. Maybe the moment is ripe for a TED Talk devoted to French rhythmic groups, if that doesn't already exist. It would get a lot of attention if it helped learners appreciate how essential those groups are to being understood, but would it help them progress? Whether sensitivity to rhythm in language is innate or something you can master with good instruction and enough determination is a big question. Did you learn about the packaging of words in school?

C If you think of language as music, then yes, "innate" can describe sensitivity to rhythm in the same way it describes musical talent. But the answer to the "big question" essentially lies in immersion. The more exposure one has, the more permeable one is to a new beat, and the more adept one becomes at fine-tuning it.

Now let me turn the question around to you. How did you learn where to place stress in English words? Why, for instance, stress the second syllable in "pronounce" but the fourth in "pronunciation"?

L The longer I look at these words, the stranger they appear. How or when I learned to emphasize the final syllable in "pronounce" is a mystery. It's weird that an old Irving Berlin tune in the play *Annie Get Your Gun* just popped into my mind. The lyrics make a point about school learning versus "doin' what comes naturally," but there's nothing intuitive about what syllables to emphasize in English. Or in French. I'll leave it to the specialists to duke it out.

C Phoneticians may argue over what should be considered the norm, but it mostly trickles down from what they hear, observe, and painstakingly transcribe. Except for them, and language teachers who must grasp the rules of the language they've been speaking all along,

"IL A NEIGÉ"

C A poem that still comes to mind on snowy days. I was seven and a blond little girl when I recited it for the first time, swinging from one foot to the other in my mother's class.

Il a neigé

Il a neigé dans l'aube rose,
Si doucement neigé
Que le chaton noir croit rêver.
C'est à peine s'il ose
Marcher.
Il a neigé dans l'aube rose,
Si doucement neigé
Que les choses
Semblent avoir changé.

Maurice Carême

The curvy link she had us draw between *semblent* and *avoir* in the last sentence signaled a *liaison* to be made for the sake of rhythm. For once the oddly silent -*ent* verb ending, cause of countless public stumbles, became sound. It was revenge as much as music.

people don't learn what they grew up hearing — they just "know" it.

And by the way, there's nothing not to like about your ability to pick up speech patterns. It is a gift, and why *chui* found a home with you.

L For which I'm grateful. I've never thought of this gift in pedagogical terms, but maybe I should. When I taught fiction classes, I urged my students to keep in mind the things they did well, as these are easily forgotten when you're focused solely on what needs work.

But back to "rhythmic groups." Tell me how you get this idea across to your students.

C   By painting the French soundscape as often as I can, particularly at the beginner's level when ears are still young. One idea, one group, one breath: learning where to pause is learning that rhythm and meaning go hand in hand. Adjectives belong with the nouns they qualify, verbs with their subject pronouns, etc. Students look for, trip over, and move boundaries until rhythmic groups form naturally, as do the sounds squeezed within.

L   You mean the "pshh pshh pshh" business, or whatever else we named it.

C   That business has an actual name: *euphonie*. Etymologically, "good voice." In concrete terms, sounds that are nice to the ear and easy to pronounce. It calls for the dropping of the E's that get in the way — your slithery *chui* is a direct result of *euphonie* — and the *liaisons* and *élisions* that smooth it all out. No creaky breaks is rule number one.

L   I must have been trying to do away with those creaky breaks back in my New York days when I mispronounced the name of the late Anthony Bourdain's restaurant Les Halles. Pronounced correctly, that H almost sticks in your throat, like a piece of food that won't go up or down. I slid the two words together instead for a more palatable sound. That seemed fitting for a great brasserie, but my friends had no idea what restaurant I was talking about. I can try to memorize words beginning with *H aspiré* until I'm ready to *hurler*, but the blank look on my pals' faces provided a quick pronunciation lesson that stuck with me.

C   *Le H aspiré* is a hard one to swallow but without it, teachers like to say, "*les héros sont des zéros*." Think of this example as your Heimlich maneuver.

L   How do they manage *l'on* versus *on*? Some of my notes from the Carlyle days show what a big one that was for me. At first I thought using *l'on* when *on* would do perfectly well was writerly signposting meant to indicate I was reading Literature with a capital L. Later I discarded that idea and decided it was about *euphonie* and flow. Having

SEPT MOTS QUI EN DISENT LONG

C "Pronounce these seven words properly in French, and you're well on your way to speaking the language." Encouraging if not bold. The online *Collins Dictionary* offers a short, crowded tour of French pronunciation. *Restaurant* features the raspy French R, a nasal vowel, and a silent consonant, *café crème* the accents *aigu* and *grave*. *Haute couture* flaunts an extravagant H *aspiré*, silent final E's, and the dubious u/ou pair. *Magnifique* throws the spotlight on "gn" and "qu," and a fancy *concierge* exhibits a C pronounced two different ways. Even fancier, *Monsieur* sounds nothing like he looks. The tour closes with *œil de bœuf* (literally "bull's eye"), the ornate round or oval window often found peeking out of a gray French roof, starring two *E's dans l'O* and the semivowel [j].

Feeling maxed out on pronunciation tips? *Encore un effort* please. There are only two more items to go, each as useful to enthusiasts of French *art de vivre* as the first seven.

Mastering the soft whistle of a C *cédille* is *de rigueur* when asking a *garçon* to check on your order. So is adding *s'il vous plaît*. The accent capping the I is a friendly reminder, as are all *accents circonflexes*, of an S sacrificed hundreds of years ago and remodeled into the so-called *chapeau chinois*. In the Middle Ages, people pleaded with *s'il vus plaist*. And their *crespes* must have looked like ours today. The word came from the twelfth-century adjective *cresp*, meaning curly or wavy and suggestive of the shape *crêpes* can take when they blister. By the way, *E accent circonflexe* is the only crowned vowel to sound different from its plain counterpart. "The exception confirms the rule" applies to pronunciation more than anything else.

noticed how often — and eloquently — it's used on TV5 has persuaded me that it can be about both. But I did come across one pointer I think I can retain.

C Anything I can share with my students?

L You probably already have. Using *l'on* to avoid an unfortunate hiatus makes me laugh. How many times have I said *qu'on* without realizing it can be mistaken for *con*? *L'on* to the rescue.

C   Very few, I'm sure: context and intonation must have cleared confused minds. But for good measure, here is our rescuer in action: *Que l'on ait parlé de rythme*, and that we only talked about rhythm so far is understandable given the impact it has on sounds. However, vowels and consonants deserve closer attention.

L   Context and intonation make me think of the pool that came with our rented house in France. I inherited a crew of boys from the suburbs of Paris who became my son's summer pals. They spent the summer with grandmothers or uncles who lived in our neighborhood and appeared like magic every afternoon at *quatorze heures pile* in their swimming trunks.

By then I had friends, too, and one of them was Marie-Claire. Our daughters were very fond of each other and I got lucky with this smart and outspoken mom. She shortened a name she'd never liked to Marie *tout court* and it suited her. One afternoon she gave me what I believed was a compliment on my summer blond hair and I thanked her.

"Dis donc, Linda, tu as plein de cheveux blancs!"

Blancs, blonds, blancs, blonds. The words sounded alike to my untrained ear, but when and how did I figure out the difference between white hairs and blond South of France streaks? Did understanding take place days or weeks after Marie left, or did I finally get it once I returned to the States and colored my hair for the first time? The question of time and context interests me almost as much as the substance of what I learned.

C   Language stories make great learning tools. Some of the best ones I've heard, told, or lived happen to be pronunciation moments. I have yet to dare ask students whether they're complimenting me on my ass or thanking me sometimes — *Merci. Beau cul!* is only one vowel away from *Merci beaucoup!* I guess I'll refrain, although no doubt my asking would give the u/ou distinction fresh meaning.

L   I don't think we made too many of those glitches at The Carlyle, unless you remember differently. But there was plenty of exposure to the French soundscape. The lessons I retain are the pop-up ones that I didn't see coming. They didn't always occur during our lunches, but when they did they were welcome.

"Qui veut lire un passage?"

It's one thing to track down the meaning of words, and quite another to pronounce them properly. I was glad Anne volunteered to go first.

She was always sensitive to the delicate balancing act of being heard by our table, but not our neighbor's. Anne read with the *élan* of a true lover of French literature. She was in the midst of a passage from the novel she had chosen for our group, *Le boulevard périphérique*, by Belgian author Henry Bauchau, when you pointed out the distinction between *tu* and *tout*.

"Tu entends la différence?"

The learning moment triggered an inadvertent exercise as Anne repeated *tu* and *tout* back-to-back several times.

C   Did you *"tutou"* too?

HENRY BAUCHAU

L   A physician herself, Anne's attraction to the work of Belgian psychiatrist Henry Bauchau was no mystery. The story unfolds as the narrator travels *le périphérique*, the beltway separating central Paris from the working-class *banlieues*, to visit his daughter-in-law in a Parisian hospital. While attending to the needs of the sick in real time, he is haunted by memories of Stéphane, a friend who perished in the war, and his Nazi captor Shadow. Ninety-five years old at the time of the book's publication, Bauchau eloquently examines the past and present in life and in death, as well as the psychological ring roads that separate them. *Le périphérique* continues to be a powerful image for writers. We'll revisit it in our chapter on films.

L   Yes, by practicing the sounds later in front of a mirror. My face looked the same on the surface, like nothing terribly important was going on. *Tu* only sounded right if I slid my tongue forward slightly in a stiff position. To give *tout* the nice pop it needed meant loosening my tongue and kind of dropping it down with an aspiration of air.

C I may quote you next time French vowels are up for discussion in class. "Like nothing terribly important is going on" is a fair description of what actually goes on to produce distinct *voyelles à la française*: tension in the mouth and jaw, along with the proper position of the lips and tongue. Stretched, puckered, or neutral lips make a crucial difference, the only one, to give but one example, to distinguish between rice (*riz*), street (*rue*), and rat (*rat*). Add a retracting tongue and streets will turn into wheels (*roue*). And mind that opening of the mouth for, if a tad wider, a burp (*rot*) will sound.

L Saying *riz, rue, rat, roue, rot* properly and in quick succession demands a kind of rigidity. It also gives the lower half of my face a workout that I find energizing. Contorting the tongue and the mouth

IPA: THE ALPHABET, NOT THE BEER

C But happy hours all the same — for learners of French *surtout*. The alternative to decoding letters is reading transcriptions of sounds, and when thirty-seven sounds have more than 130 spellings, that is not a choice to take lightly.

The International Phonetic Alphabet is a comprehensive set of symbols for all of the sounds of spoken languages. Some are unique to one language, others common to many. [ʃ], for instance, is the sound (or phoneme) of "sh" in "shoe" and "ch" in *chaussure* since both pairs (of letters) are, in these two words, pronounced identically. Used for phonetic transcriptions, the IPA offers shortcuts to the heart of rhythmic groups: *liaisons* whiz and buzz, silent letters shush while others make new sounds.

See and try for yourself:

[ʃkrwaksɛtuskirɛst]: *Je crois que c'est tout ce qui reste.*

[sɛtynkɛstjɔ̃tstil]: *C'est une question de style.*

If you need a little push, experiment with what students refer to as "machine gun drills." Repeat a sentence faster and faster until words morph into what they should sound like — that smooth road battered by rain.

DICTÉE IMPROVISÉE

L   YouTube offers plenty of informal instruction on how to make some of the outrageously difficult sounds that comprise the French language, but stumbling upon Magali Bertin, blogger and makeup maven, was a revelation. I found her by searching for the expression *point trop n'en faut* (which warns us not to go too far), and wound up hooked on her tutorials on *makeup de mystère*. The beauty tips are great and who wouldn't want to know about *le fameux trois*, an application of blush at the temples, cheeks, and jawline? What's more riveting is the plasticity of Bertin's face as she applies various cosmetics. Yes, she hams it up with campy gestures emphasizing her generous mouth and wide eyes. But theatricality is a boon to correct pronunciation. The rolling R's or glides, those not-quite vowels inherent in *oui* [wi] or *loi* [lwa], require fortitude to pronounce, but a stiff upper lip will get you nowhere fast.

In the mood to misappropriate a rollicking *dictée* with Bernard Pivot? His televised dictation competitions to improve spelling and grammar remain a popular national pastime. My score on one of his *dictées* meant I wouldn't be passing my *bac* anytime soon. Then I thought of the lovely lilt he gave to the word *rimailleurs*. How great would that be if I could make those same sounds? Improvising a quick lesson in elocution from the *maître* of literary broadcast television turned out to be fairly easy. Listening to Pivot's televised words on my computer, pushing pause, then recording myself as I repeated them into an iPhone gave me pause. My pronunciation hardly matched his, but I had a good time mimicking the master.

and the particular angle of the jaw are sensual elements that make the act of speaking French feel organic and alive.

Have you ever heard of Long Island lockjaw? The stiff-jawed way of speaking in which the mouth and lips barely move has been variously labelled Locust Valley lockjaw, boarding school lockjaw, and who knows what else. Regardless of what it's called, would you consider this a handicap or an advantage when it comes to speaking French?

C   Locked jaws can be an asset when coupled with flapping lips. The French are *spécialistes* in combining the two.

WHAT DO YOU MEAN ...

C ... the wind is good? *Pas le vent, le vin!*

The very French nasal vowels (nonexistent in many languages) must be handled with care. Confusing one with another can obscure or distort meaning, especially with monosyllabic words.

Not nasalizing a vowel has similar consequences: it can, to name but two examples, change ends into facts: [fɛ̃] *fin* → [fɛ] *fait* or funds into scythes: [fɔ̃] *fonds* → [fo] *faux*. (Reminder: the signs in square brackets are phonetic transcriptions of the French words — as you'll notice, nasal vowels are represented with a tilde on top.)

Now please pinch your nose and say [gɑ̃] *gants*. Vibrations along the walls of the nose mean the air is going through. Not until you're feeling that buzz will gloves truly be gloves [gɑ̃] and not guys [ga] *gars*.

Ready for some action? Hop from one nasal vowel to the next, then alternate: nasal, oral, nasal, oral ... Let's start with the letter B: [bɔ̃] *bon*, [bɑ̃] *banc*, [bɛ̃] *bain*. Then [bɔ̃] *bon* / [bo] *beau*, [bɑ̃] *banc* / [ba] *bas*, [bɛ̃] *bain* / [bɛ] *baie*. Continue with L: [lɔ̃] *long*, [lɑ̃] *lent*, [lɛ̃] *lin*. Then [lɔ̃] *long* / [lo] *l'eau*, [lɑ̃] *lent* / [la] *là*, [lɛ̃] *lin* / [lɛ] *lait*. And P: [pɔ̃] *pont*, [pɑ̃] *pend*, [pɛ̃] *pain*. Then [pɔ̃] *pont* / [po] *pot*, [pɑ̃] *pend* / [pa] *pas*, [pɛ̃] *pain* / [pɛ] *paix*.

Repeat the exercise with more letters — and expand your collection of *petits mots*.

L What would you say is the most challenging *règle* for students?

C "Don't call it like you see it." The twenty-six letters of the French alphabet make thirty-seven sounds, which have more than 130 different spellings. Heads of garlic, heights, and water have one thing in common in French, and that is the way they sound: *aulx, hauts*, and *eau*, each a sharp O — pure madness for speakers of languages where pronunciation matches spelling.

L Are *hauts* ever pronounced "hots" by students?

C More often than you'd think. Silent letters are their *bête noire* — and my own, though one recent trespass was worth enduring dozens. A dried fruit lover, calling attention to the health benefits of his favorite snack, proclaimed, "*J'adore les fruits secs!*" That his last loud S made them a special superfood didn't help get the point across, but I couldn't have cared less.

Final E's seem most irresistible — and confusing — in verbal forms. To pronounce them when they should be silent is to go back in time: *je parle* then sounds like the past form *je parlais* or like *parler*, the timeless infinitive.

L This would be something you'd stop a conversation for and correct?

C I would for this and whatever hinders intelligibility, not for signs of foreignness that coat meaning but don't alter it. An American R rolling its way into a French word does not cause ambiguity, only smiles. If the first attempts to correct it prove difficult, *je le laisse rouler.* Time and practice will run their course — and that is not simply an easy way out.

L Do students ever disagree with you?

C I learned the hard way about overcorrecting. The only horrendous feedback I received was years ago from a student

OURRRRHHHH

C "'Ourrrrhhhh.'

Je croyais connaître la cuisine japonaise, mais cela, je n'avais jamais entendu. Je lui demandai de m'expliquer. Sobrement, il répéta:

'Ourrrrhhhh.'

Oui, certes, mais qu'était-ce?"

Like Amélie Nothomb, I could not have made sense of the "word" without a clue. Not until Rinri, the young man she is teaching to speak French, draws an egg do either of us understand what he enjoys eating. By the end of his first private class, the Tokyoite's pronunciation shifts, if not in the right direction, at least towards something different. A more distinct (and predictable) shift occurs between the two when French lessons turn into the love affair the Belgian author recounts with theatrical flair in her autobiographical novel *Ni d'Ève ni d'Adam*. The book's opening sentence — "The most efficient way to learn Japanese, it seemed, would be to teach French" — is spot-on.

(whose handwriting I recognized) taking revenge on the systematic corrections I thought would help her equally horrendous pronunciation. They must have been torture to her — the only plausible explanation for the condescending anger she expressed about me to the administration, and a fierce reminder that clear, natural pronunciation is beyond what is expected of even a fluent speaker.

L   Good to know. I can't tell you how many times I've heard non-native speakers of French apologize for their "terrible accents." I guess the assumption is that I've got this nailed since I once lived there.

C   "Pronunciation is clearly intelligible even if a foreign accent is sometimes evident and occasional mispronunciations occur" is the definition of phonological control for the CEFR B1 level, considered the threshold of fluency. It is also what, on most days, defines my own control of English pronunciation with — or despite — thirty years of practice and a good pair of ears. Both the CEFR description and my personal experience help decide whether or not phonetic corrections are worth interrupting an otherwise flowing sentence.

Speaking of flow, you may be surprised how much real interactions "unclog" pronunciation. A level one student certainly was, when, after rounds of maimed *nationalités* (she kept pronouncing the word *à l'américaine*), it popped out just fine the moment when she truly was interested in her classmates' origins. I had a similar experience with the Arabic *qaf* (as challenging to me as the French R is to Americans) which did sound right the day I exchanged a few words with a Qatari man on the bus. My textbook had triggered his curiosity. Our spontaneous back-and-forth, my first in Arabic, marked a clear step toward autonomy.

L   Now you've got me thinking about autonomy in another sense. Stumbling upon Alliance Française de Los Angeles changed the way I practiced French post–New York. I began by taking literature classes and the monthly book group I now attend has been a real lifeline. Have I lost my independence as a learner by doing so? I'd like to think reading literature and talking about it in a quasi-classroom enhances it.

Nadine, who teaches at Alliance, uses a judicious touch when offering pronunciation corrections as we read aloud or speak about the books we've read. I wouldn't be surprised if your guidelines were hers as well: Does it have an impact on intelligibility? Is it worth interrupting the flow? It's a mighty task to facilitate a monthly book group open to any and all. Coaxing the shy ones to speak at all can be taxing. I know, since I am one myself.

C A colleague once called pronunciation *le parent pauvre de l'enseignement*. Why it receives little to no attention at advanced levels is a mystery, given the importance it has in relation to fluency.

L Didn't you just say mispronunciations and a foreign accent were OK?

C Provided they don't thwart communication. I will quote the CEFR again: pronunciation should be "clearly intelligible." Please watch the trailer of *L'élégance du hérisson*, and tell me what you think of M. Ozu's French.

L It threw me off balance. This wasn't the M. Ozu I knew from reading the book.

C A model of eloquence — but only on paper. His movie doppelgänger speaks a French so raspy that for a moment, I wondered whether he was a Helen Marsh–type character, or infatuated with *H aspirés*. My guesses proved to be wrong — and not even funny when I learned the actor spoke zero French prior to the shoot. His coach should have worked on rhythmic groups rather than throaty R's.

L It's unfair to contrast Togo Igawa's delivery with fellow actor Bradley Cooper's apparent ease in speaking the language since Cooper lived with a French family in Aix-en-Provence as a student, but I'm doing it anyway. Cooper's laid-back French is a pleasure, even though his grammar and vocab may not be as pristine as M. Ozu's.

C Grammar expertise plus a wide range of vocabulary plus labored pronunciation equal bad news. Unfortunate, but nonetheless true: spoken language doesn't flow without clear pronunciation.

L   So back to my question: Why is pronunciation not given more attention in class?

C   The ability to hear and reproduce sounds goes beyond practice. It is also a question of desire — or fear. At least I think so, and since I may well be the only one, I will speak for myself. Fantasies or representations of Americans and American culture — whether I identify with or reject them — permeate how I sound, much more than how I write or read. Pronunciation is the intimate part of language learning. It involves physicality, the use of body parts that the intellect alone cannot control; it is a place where deeper, more subtle currents are at work — where slips of the tongue make literal sense, where accents and errors may also be unconscious choices.

You mentioned the sensuality of the act of speaking French. That tells me how comfortable you are being French.

L   It all depends on the crowd. Had makers of a plastic pouch in a Tulsa drugstore capitalized on its Old Northern French spelling by naming it a pouche? I'll never know, but a friend thought I was putting on airs and trying to "be all sophisticated" when I called it a *pouché*. That might have been an accurate charge once I got to college, but this was high school and the accusation stung. To this day I hesitate about whether to pronounce something as it's meant to be pronounced in French or Americanize it to avoid sounding affected. *Croissant* or craw-sont? Either way it's a minefield of awkward possibilities.

C   How does the new-sounding self abide with the existing one? Peacefully I hope. Pronunciation may well be acculturation at its most compelling.

L   Thank you for not being sure. Accommodating a new-sounding self may mean coming up with ideas that aren't fully formed, though without them there would be no adventure in learning. Or in this exchange. This was a hard chapter, but worth it.

C   Ready for a break? *Unptiblanfrai, satdi?*

L   I wouldn't say no to a glass of chardonnay about now. *À la tienne!* ❦

6

Louder Than Words
Mais en douceur

LINDA: Don't tell me you're taking back what you said about the importance of vocabulary.

C Not at all, but sounding French, grammar, vocabulary, and clear pronunciation are not enough.

L I'm still recovering from the last chapter.

C I trust a discussion of *savoir-faire* and *savoir-être* will bring your energy back up.

L Let's clarify those terms first. Are you talking about sophistication?

C *Adresse* or *habileté* are better terms. You can have all the language in the world, but without knowing how to communicate, no one will hear you. Beaumarchais said: "*Pour gagner du bien, le savoir-faire vaut mieux que le savoir.*"

L Where is this maxim taking us?

C Listen to this story. A few years ago, I found myself arguing over Goodwill Ambassadors.

"*Et pensez-vous que les prises de position politiques de Yannick Noah soient compatibles avec les fonctions d'Ambassadeur de bonne volonté?*"

"Oui, absolument. Un grand nombre d'Ambassadeurs de bonne volonté expriment librement leurs opinions politiques. C'est leur droit. S'ils le font avec respect, c'est même un devoir envers la jeunesse qu'ils représentent."

My attempt to make a meager point failed. Not once in the ten minutes of our exchange was I able to sway *mon interlocutrice.* So I caved. Yes, Yannick Noah would make a better UNESCO Goodwill Ambassador than Julien Clerc, two French celebrities equally suited for the job, or so I fancied until her argument won me over.

The conversation would have been quite unpleasant had it happened at a party but in the …

L   *Pardon si je t'interromps.* This reminds me of an evening in France during an American election. I must have been expressing some fairly fervent opinions. Our host leaned back on his sofa during the discussion that took place after the meal. Peering at me through a cloud of cigarette smoke, he reminded me that this was dinner, *pas la guerre.* I don't remember what I was defending so vehemently, but I do recall the smile on his face as he explained *les règles du jeu.* I've since come to understand that a certain playfulness goes a long way in France.

C   *J'imagine qu'ailleurs aussi* — just not in the room where I was deep in conversation with a student (before you interrupted me). Our exchange was no dinner talk but part of an oral exam, and under these circumstances war was rather fun — in fact impressive. My examinee showed a command of repartee and a solid *esprit de synthèse.* She had had to process a substantial amount of information about the two men (available to her in written, audio, and video documents) and was able, each time I questioned her chosen candidate's suitability for the position, to pull out the one piece that undermined my point while defending hers with confidence.

As she left the room, she asked if the oral part of the exam would count for as much as the written part. Yes, it will, I answered. Her enquiry, and relief at my response, confirmed the assessment of her skills: average command of the language (which would blatantly show on paper) along with excellent reading, listening, and pragmatic skills. Despite grammar blunders (corrected in the transcription of her response above) and a range of vocabulary largely informed by her native Spanish, the memory I have of her is that of a formidable speaker, able to not only engage in but lead the interaction and do so with clarity, coherence, and relative ease. She succeeded by making the best possible practical use of her limited French.

L   I've never thought of this as *savoir-faire*. My turn for another story.

During the thirty-odd minutes I spent on the telephone with Yvette Caël in 2001 I didn't once worry about whether or not to use an inversion with my questions instead of *est-ce que*, nor did I fret about my failure to properly use the subjunctive. I wasn't thinking about French at all because I was too busy speaking it. My husband's book on the 442nd Regiment, the Japanese American battalion that fought in World War II, was on the line, and Mme Caël was refusing my request for an interview with her husband. I sat on the edge of the bed in a hotel in Gérardmer and begged shamelessly, pulling out every stop. We had come all the way from New York and driven up from Nice, following the course of the Rhône to retrace the footsteps of the soldiers her husband had risked his life to support. The war had been fought in his tiny mountain community near the border of Germany and any memories the former scout for the Resistance would be willing to share were invaluable to my husband's research. While he understood some French, my husband wasn't conversant in the language. Securing and conducting an interview would be up to me.

I carried on and on with pleas and assurances until at last Mme Caël sighed deeply and changed course.

"*Bon. Mais pas pour longtemps.*"

She explained that her husband had been ill and I promised we wouldn't linger, a promise we kept, but not in a way I could have foreseen.

The next afternoon we followed a winding road to their property, a very modest farmhouse dwarfed by the surrounding slopes. A pitched battle in October 1944 had taken place in the freezing rain and darkness just

A WAR MEMORY

C My mother remembers the day she first came upon toothpaste:

"*Sur les genoux d'un soldat américain, j'avais dix ans, cela se passait en novembre 1944. Dans ma main une petite brosse; dans la main du soldat un tube ... Qu'allait-il se passer? Un peu de pâte sort du tube et s'étale sur la* brush. Mouth *béante et* teeth *découvertes. Brossage énergique puis rinçage à l'évier de la cuisine. Quel étonnement! Mes dents sont lisses, ma bouche est parfumée ...*

Thank you *à mon inoubliable soldat.*"

beyond the house where Maurice still lived.

The soft-spoken couple welcomed us and showed us to the table in their kitchen, a large room that served double duty as a garage. I translated my husband's questions as best I could. A transcript of that meeting reveals brief questions and answers that were briefer still. About twenty minutes into the interview, Maurice Caël looked out the window of his kitchen-garage and began to cry. He hadn't spoken of the battle that had taken place in his backyard for almost sixty years, and his tears provided a radical context for translation as he relived the battle. We didn't ask further questions as more tea was served. Years later, my husband received an eloquent letter of thanks from M. Caël for his copy of *Just Americans*.

C What a fabulous story.

L It remains one of the most powerful experiences in the French language I've ever had. Securing Mme Caël's permission to speak with her husband wasn't frivolous. This was a very real component of my husband's enterprise. There was no occasion to gloat about leaping over a language barrier, although I did feel pride at putting my skills to concrete use.

C And proud you should be. I well imagine the elderly woman set in her quiet rural ways to have been wary of American writers, the first and only ones she and her frail husband would likely meet. Your ability to lay a path into their home and emotionally charged past speaks volumes to your *savoir-faire* — and *savoir-être*. I bet that "shameless begging" was tinged with charm, patience, and empathy, not to mention insight.

SAVOIR-ÊTRE OU NE PAS SAVOIR-ÊTRE

C That is indeed the question — *même pour les plus grands*. Former French president Nicolas Sarkozy learned it the hard way. Google "French insult *con*" and the "*Casse-toi, pauvre con!*" he yelled to a man who turned down his handshake makes it to the top of the page. The invective gave rise to an international debate over its meaning but whatever translation one settles on, from "Buzz off, loser!" or "Get lost, you idiot!" to an overblown "Fuck you, prick!," it's safe to say that none suits a *chef d'État*. Nor does *racaille*, the term he used, this time as interior minister, to describe French rioters. What, the world pondered, did he mean? Scumbags or just rabble?

Sarkozy's temper hurt him; his lifestyle did the rest. A victory dinner attended by the richest and most powerful at the swishy Champs-Elysées restaurant Le Fouquet's is not how the French expect their president to celebrate his coming to power, particularly when the party continues on board the yacht of a billionaire businessman. Within his first week in office, Sarkozy had become President Bling-Bling. And in 2007, there was no Donald Trump to eclipse him yet — in the temper or glitz department.

L Your student and I had something in common: she needed to win your argument to pass the exam and I needed to get my husband an interview for his book. There's nothing like having something at stake to bring your *savoir-faire* up to speed.

Savoir-être seems the more elusive term. The only similar expression that comes to mind in English is interpersonal skills, and that's way too corporate.

C One translation given for *savoir-être* is existential competence, which, in line with its philosophical reference, describes personal identity (attitudes, motivations, values, cognitive styles, and personality types) as a key factor in communication.

Social interaction, oral or written, relies on teamwork: language experts fix language bugs, communication strategists decide on what to say, how,

LEÇON DE VIE

C   Monsieur Bark and Monsieur Linh, two gentlemen I had the joy of becoming acquainted with in Philippe Claudel's novel *La petite fille de Monsieur Linh*, are embodiments of *savoir-être* and remarkable teachers of the subject. An old man haunted by memories of his war-torn country, Monsieur Linh lives in a foreign land where he brought his infant granddaughter to safety. Culture shock and isolation make life as a refugee a daunting task until his encounter with the sympathetic and equally alone Monsieur Bark. A three-word repertoire is no barrier to the two men finding solace and more in each other's company. The willingness to develop a human relationship, along with a watchful and curious eye, pave the way to friendship. They learn the language of looks, tones, and gestures and learn it well, so well their unlikely dialogue is a powerful *leçon de vie*.

and when to say it. Both operate in tandem in each one of us, ideally with equal weight. Good language skills do not make up for poor *savoir-être*. How often do I cut a conversation short when my interlocutors are bores or fanfarons? *Souvent.* And when no escape is in sight, the option to morph into a silent nodding presence is always available.

L   Like so many writers, I spend a disproportionate amount of time in a room staring at my computer. I ask plenty of questions when I escape that room and my own thoughts. Might my communication style come across as invasive in France, especially in business situations?

C   Not if your questions are interesting and to the point — and if you leave others, business people included, time to ask their own. My father must have had many when he travelled the world in search of new markets. I was a little, and very puzzled, girl, when I heard him say *sentir le marché* for the first time. The only *marché* I knew was the one at place du Général de Gaulle, where, on Saturday mornings, we'd buy fruits and vegetables. What on earth was Dad doing abroad smelling, or worse, touching food stands? *Savoir-apprendre* is what I read into the phrase today. The ability to observe, process, and interpret cultural practices gave him insight into foreign dress codes and the colors, designs, and textile blends to serve them best. *Savoir-apprendre* was his power tool, and paired with social intuition, resulted in great success.

A PHOTOGRAPH

C   One which, among the many on display in my father's office, catches the eye. It was taken some thirty years ago in Inner Mongolia in the north of China. My dad wears a business suit, and his burgundy tie is the only splash of color amidst the dusty hues of the arid, windblown patch of land where he stands. Next to him is a shepherd clad in a long sheepskin coat and heavy boots. The unusual pair poses, circled by a flock of cashmere goats grazing at the sparse, dry grass, and with their big, genuine smiles could pass for longtime friends. But smiles were all they could exchange. Even the fluent Mandarin of Dad's agent (the photographer) was of no help in the attempt to communicate.

In the early '80s, my father ran a textile factory for which he started working as a fourteen-year-old paycheck delivery boy, riding his bike to bring the weavers working from home in the surrounding small towns their wages. In thirty years, his responsibilities had grown as the European textile industry declined. He well understood the need to create new products and his search for ideas and new fibers first took him to China, where he discovered their cashmere wool. Along with creative designs and innovative weaving techniques, cashmere made the firm's renown.

L   I've only met your dad once, but he seemed very comfortable in a raucous New York restaurant, far from Alsace. He read the scene right away and I'm not just talking about the menu. I'll bet you could plop him down anywhere and he'd be making lasting connections in no time.

C   The New Year's cards they exchanged again last December, twenty years into retirement, salute the relationship my father and Mr. Kuwahara, the firm's agent in Japan, developed over time — and over dinners in each other's homes. How many did it take for the strange to become familiar, for my father to enjoy Mrs. Kuwahara's food knowing she would dine alone in a separate room, or for Mr. Kuwahara to understand that our "dirty" — his word — German shepherd was family? Language alone — both spoke basic English — cannot explain how each eased into the other's world. Both also were able to decenter — to stop placing their own culture and expectations *au centre*.

JOHNNY

L   Although I was always up for a French film, I didn't get my husband's over-the-top excitement about a movie called *Man on the Train* in the spring of 2003. He filled in some blanks about one of the stars who was both a singer and an actor as we hurried to the tiny theater half a block from our apartment. A French friend once dismissed Johnny Hallyday as being *un peu trop spectacle* and I didn't think to ask whether she meant his concerts or his life. My husband looked increasingly aghast.

"How can you have lived in France all that time and not know about Johnny?"

The film opened with the twang of a guitar, suggesting the lawless American frontier. The minute Johnny strode into the French village, as menacing as a gunslinger in a John Ford film, I was as smitten as Jean Rochefort, who played a retired literature teacher in the provinces. Johnny's taciturn edge and icy blue eyes suggested a violent edge just barely kept in check. This stranger to town straddled two worlds, the American West and France, a motif that resonated throughout the movie. Every silence, every minimalist gesture pointed to a deep knowledge of the two cultures. Where did Johnny truly belong? And what was up with that American name? The learning experience launched that night would prove to be as kooky as it was intense.

My quest involved catching up with what most of France already knew. I combed the Internet for videotapes of his films and performances that took weeks to ship. I breathlessly opened the blue *faux* lizard cover of his autobiography called *Destroy* and became increasingly unmoored as I discovered the depth of his connection to my hometown. Born Jean-Philippe Smet, the rocker adopted the moniker of his mentor and father figure, Lee Halliday, a dancer in the stage play of *Oklahoma!* who first met young Jean-Philippe, his aunt, and cousins in London. Finding out that Lee, who provided him with his first cowboy outfit and would go on to marry his cousin, had grown up in a small town adjacent to Tulsa was *le too much*, to borrow from Johnny's vernacular.

The megastar never appeared to outgrow his fascination with American culture and the West. It was very affecting to take a brief Internet trip down Route 66 with a much older, badass Johnny and his band of French biker *potes*. "*Regarde ce paysage au lieu de me regarder moi*," Johnny urges one of his fellow travelers, and for a few moments, I tried to do the same.

L *Décentré* or *dépaysé*? Can you be one without the other?

C *Le dépaysement* is an instinctive response to being out of place when the environment looks, sounds, and smells different. But it takes curiosity to reflect on the strange and not just react to it — it takes even more to question the familiar. *Et j'en suis la preuve*: thirty years as a French New Yorker haven't softened all of the blows. I've grown to understand that asking for information requires no greetings, no "excuse me" — and certainly no conditional mood — on the streets of New York, yet there are times when a blunt "Is Montague Street this way?" startles me as much as someone stepping through my doorway without a knock.

L Your visceral reaction is exactly what Canadian writers Julie Barlow and Jean-Benoît Nadeau describe in *The Bonjour Effect: The Secret Codes of French Conversation Revealed*. Their yearlong stay in Paris provided them with endless fodder for the book. Why was Jean-Benoît accused of being *mal élevé* by a bus driver after boarding a bus? He had forgotten a ritual he knew well, that's why. Saying *bonjour* — and saying it with civility — is like opening a magic door in France. The polite convention is mandatory, and as your experience suggests, doesn't vanish just because you've left the mother country.

My take on things is different. I don't find a question about directions off-putting or even impolite. Anytime a stranger approaches me with a sunny hello, I'm primed to be asked for a donation, a signature, or some

> **BREAKING UP IN STYLE**
>
> **C** Much worse than an unwanted *tu* is an unwanted *vous*. The last words of Serge Gainsbourg's "Lost Song," a tale of forsaken love, deal the *coup de grâce*. And only "France's premier pop poet" could have dealt it so gracefully:
>
> *Je reconnais je me suis vue*
>
> *À l'avance battue*
>
> *C'est l'horreur mais ton*
>
> *Arrogance me tue*
>
> *Tu me dis vous après tu*

LESSON LEARNED

L Exuberant French floated in the air and foreign camera crews panned the crowded sidewalk outside the Orpheum Theatre. It was April 24, 2012, and Johnny Hallyday was about to play Los Angeles for the first time.

It was Francophile heaven inside the stately theater. A blond Johnny clone strode past in a leather jacket emblazoned with the image of a lone wolf and my husband counted the number of men with pastel sweaters tossed over their shoulders. If there were other Americans present, I didn't see them that night.

"This is like a party I wasn't invited to," my DJ son muttered.

An older woman with a frizzy mop of hair plopped down in the row before us. She brushed the squared shoulders of her suit and huffed as a group slid past to their seats, but boundaries dissolved as the theater filled with increasingly animated French.

"*Ah non,*" she corrected the man next to her. "*C'est masculin.*"

An exchange about grammar followed. The woman then shifted to another topic and all at once they were in the land of *tu*. Was it grammar or Johnny fever that provoked the shift to the familial? The theater was packed now and people turned to wave frantically at someone in the balcony. Cameras flashed. Was Johnny mingling with his fans in this intimate venue? I leaned forward to launch my burning question.

"*C'est lui?*"

The woman gave me a hard stare and said nothing.

"*Est-ce que c'est Johnny là-haut?*"

"I don't know."

I kept my eye on the back of the woman's suit as the lights dimmed. She had given me the coldest shoulder of all with her refusal to answer in French, deflecting my American accent and whatever presumptions she heard in my question. I thought of his 699-page autobiography, as a black silhouette appeared onstage. Did she know that Johnny had once lied to reporters and told them he'd been raised on a ranch in Oklahoma by an American father? I felt entitled to my passion for Johnny and was in too much of a snit to put the *savoir-faire* and *savoir-être* I'd learned in France to any use.

Months later I still hadn't gotten the memo. A trainer at Gold's Gym knew of my fascination with Johnny Hallyday and pointed him out to me as the star was winding up a call on his cell. Maybe if I'd begun with *bonjour* things would have turned out differently. Instead I rushed ahead with praise for his concert in tremulous French. Johnny was good enough to shake the hand I extended, although he remained utterly silent. Not only had I trespassed on his private space, I'd blown the cover of a star who lived for the most part incognito in Los Angeles. I never saw him again at Gold's and eventually dropped my membership at the gym.

Johnny's death in 2017 produced a tidal wave of mourning among his lifelong fans. I wondered whether the question in the title of an early film *D'où viens-tu Johnny?* had ever been truly answered and whether it even mattered to those faithful followers.

variant of both. I feel much more inclined to help if someone begins with a simple "excuse me."

C   Exchanges like this one should take place routinely in language courses. The *tu/vous* distinction is the first, and rare, chance students have to understand that sometimes culture matters more than grammar. So I don't hesitate to stretch it a little: to *tu* prematurely may kill a conversation before it begins.

L   I usually ask permission to move from *vous* to *tu* and haven't been told no yet. Are the French trying to spare me the pain of rebuke?

C   No. Not only is it the right thing to do, it also shows you're able to "see the picture" through French eyes. Crossing the line to a warmer, friendlier relationship is a delicate act that takes more than just applying the rules. I bet *tutoyer* Mme Caël didn't even occur to you, did it?

L Not once.

C You are interculturally competent, *ma chère*. That means you can switch selves, yours with your interlocutor's.

L Donna Tartt touched on this phenomenon in her novel *The Goldfinch*. "It was interesting to see the change that came over Boris when he was speaking another language — a sort of livening, or alertness, a sense of a different and more efficient person occupying his body."

For those who don't care to switch selves, embellishing who you already are can also work. A friend of mine is an expert. During a visit to France in the '80s, Jill bridged any possible cultural divide by supersizing her French schtick for comic effect. This born performer didn't bother with decorum. Instead of *bonjour*, she produced a riff that turned out to be foolproof.

Untroubled by her linguistic challenges, my self-confident buddy dazzled wherever she went by opening each exchange with two lines she retained from her high school French: "*Je m'appelle Jill. Je me suis cassé la jambe.*" With no cast on her leg, the only thing broken by her comic delivery was the ice.

WHEN SINGING SAYS SO MUCH

L Don Draper's wife put on a real show during the fifth season of *Mad Men* when she sang "Zou bisou bisou." Megan's French is French Canadian, not that Don's male colleagues notice. The French uberbabe persona leaves women round-eyed with envy and her husband squirming with a mixture of discomfort and pride as she does a flirtatious turn in her black minidress. Comments on YouTube duke it out variously over Megan's accent, feminism, and her level of hotness, but surprisingly few actually examine the lyrics. The song went viral overnight and so did the *vous* that Megan sings to her husband as she slides her hand down the middle of her body. Who cares about the *tu/vous* question when so much else is being communicated? Not The Roots, who performed a portion of the song on *The Tonight Show* the night after the episode aired.

C Your friend is an authority in *le savoir-s'engager.*

L When addressed by her first name, she would answer, "*Tu me désires?*" for maximum effect. Weeks after she left, I was still getting questions from shopkeepers and neighbors about my *drôle d'amie américaine.* A distinct New York accent and willingness to play the clown opened more doors than a volley of earnest, elementary French ever could have.

You're no stranger to her technique, by the way. I remember a certain barbecue in Hollywood, and a certain someone with a thick French accent.

INTERCULTURAL SKILLS ACCORDING TO THE CEFR

C "Knowledge, awareness and understanding of the relation (similarities and distinctive differences) between the 'world of origin' and the 'world of the target community' produce an intercultural awareness. It is, of course, important to note that intercultural awareness includes an awareness of the regional and social diversity of both worlds. In addition to objective knowledge, intercultural awareness covers awareness of how each community appears from the perspective of the other, this often in the form of national stereotypes."

UN VRAI CADEAU

L One night in Paris I found myself seated next to another lone diner. I don't know how long it took for the conversation to begin, but it ended with a walk to her hotel in the *sixième arrondissement* for an after-dinner drink and the kind of discussion colored by the fact that we knew we would never see each other again.

She and her husband lived in the small town where they had both grown up. She described a man who was more than happy to send her to Paris every year to shop. At one point I complimented her suit, something that would never have occurred to me to wear for an evening out alone. "*Je m'habille pour honorer des autres,*" she said, delicately buttering a radish. I eventually lost her name and address, but not the cultural message she offered about presentation of self.

C   Oh my God, "Don't fœuck wiz French peeple." I couldn't resist that frog puppet.

L   This Claire was a revelation to me. How did you come up with that?

C   Well, how was I to respond to the host's sweet, witty French-bashing — encircled by cool intellectuals? I didn't have his language skills or *savoir-faire* — never mind his *grande gueule*. But I had the best French accent, and with a frog speaking on my behalf, an emancipated *savoir-être*. I was the first one surprised.

L   And it was a funny, great success.

Our French group was in for a similar surprise the night Margot took the stage at a cabaret in Greenwich Village. The elegant, bare-shouldered version of this language buddy celebrating her fiftieth birthday was a stunner. Gone were the sneakers perfect for dashing from The Carlyle to a daughter's soccer match, or the fur cap with earflaps reserved for especially frigid days. This was a Margot who had rediscovered her lovely voice after she began singing to her three children. Some of her earlier shows had been highly stylized, and a few songs seemed a wink and a nod to this slightly anachronistic form of theater. But that night, as our friend moved to French, her Belgian mother's native tongue, a very different woman emerged. The lyrics in "Chanson," by Stephen Schwartz, shifted between French and English and so did Margot's affect as she sang. Our candy wrappers announced a fifty/fifty theme as suggestive as this type A mom and closet chanteuse's performance.

Whether I'm transfixed by Margot's show in a cozy cabaret, or your own Hollywood makeover, I'm reminded that a multitude of selves can be accessed, and even accessorized, in the spaces between words. What's not to *savourer* about *le savoir*? ❧

One Piece at a Time
À la tâche

LINDA: That a language teacher places *savoir-faire* and *savoir-être* above grammar and vocabulary still comes as a surprise, although you've prepared me for it. Have you always thought this way?

 C Not until the task-based approach gained ground in language teaching was I able to acutely discern the many parts of communication, and recognize the importance of pragmatic and social skills. But you must have made that distinction — consciously or not — long before I did. Wasn't "putting French into action" your learning method when you lived in France?

 L It was sink or swim. Did I say *j'ai eu* or *j'avais* an electric shock when I was taking a shower just after our move to St. Paul? Whatever tense I used brought our neighbor the electrician and his cousin the plumber to our door right away.

There's nothing like a crisis to produce enough French to get the job done. I wouldn't wish a near-calamity on anyone, but real life can be a hothouse of learning like no classroom can.

 C Yours is a punchier version of the classic, "Tell me and I forget, teach me and I may remember, involve me and I learn," and both describe task-based learning in a nutshell. The approach is considered a major development in language instruction in that it shifted the focus of learning from knowledge to actual use. What matters is what students do with language, not what they know about it, and on this you could not agree more.

ESTOUFFADE PRINTANIÈRE

L My recent *estouffade printanière* could have used more prepping. Easter brunch with a spring *mélange* of tender vegetables promised to be festive. *Cœurs d'artichauts*, asparagus, and *petits pois* with baby carrots and turnips to brighten the blend. I'd neither tasted nor prepared *fèves* before, and this was an opportunity to do both. I skimmed the recipe and, once I shopped for the vegetables, figured it would be a snap. Wrong.

Popping the fava beans out of their outer shells was only step one. The underlying shell was tough and more popping was needed to free the delicate bean inside. Additional reading revealed that the beans could be toxic to some and the allergic reaction even has a name.

Chopping the chervil and parsley with time running out was no fun and the colorful blend of baby carrots turned the whole dish an unfortunate mauve. An SOS text to guests announced that brunch had become lunch and it would be delayed for an hour.

It tasted wonderful, once you got over the drab visuals. Better still, no one perished from favism. I will never again forget one definition of *parcourir*: skimming is not the same thing as reading (and reflecting). Best to make the distinction when company's on the way.

L Real language immersion for me is when language disappears altogether. How do you create opportunities for students to dive right in? Is that what you mean by a task?

C A task is a project that involves the use of oral or written language or both. Responding to an email, taking part in a debate, giving a presentation, writing fiction … Anything that can be imagined.

L OK, but is everyone up to it? How are beginners supposed to write or speak with the little French they know?

C They warm up to it first, and write or speak a little because only a little is asked of them. Each task is considered a learning trigger regardless of its size and complexity. Its undertaking requires that the language needed for it be available for use — therefore learned.

L   So prepping goes on prior to the task.

C   As is the case in real life. Your first time baking a *charlotte aux fraises*? Step one, find and read the recipe; step two, have the right ingredients, pots, and pans on hand; step three, get to work and, in case you promised your guests a fine dessert, be sure the *pâtissier du coin* has one in stock.

L   Good point. What if students can't do the job, or do it poorly?

C   More prepping must be called for.

L   This isn't much different from what goes on in a "regular" class then.

C   Practice is part of any course, but with task-based learning, language serves a purpose rather than being an end in itself. Grammar, vocabulary, pronunciation, etc. are all geared towards the task and its outcome.

L   How do you make students aware of this?

C   The task is disclosed with a road map to guide them through the steps along the way, and a tool kit for each step.

L   And what do you pack in that tool kit?

C   The language needed to carry out these steps.

L   The road map highlights areas of language to be explored?

C   As well as their purpose — a connection often overlooked in language instruction, particularly when the focus is on form and not function. The road map essentially answers the question many have but don't ask: "What are we learning this for?"

L   What a shame that the question is neglected. It would help to have a concrete example, along with the steps I'll need to take.

HOW TO SHINE IN CLASS

C "Because language does not have to be well-formed in order to be meaningful, it is easy to see how learners could successfully complete a task using ill-formed or undemanding language, supplemented by gesture and intonation, rather than trying out their 'cutting edge' interlanguage." I share this concern, expressed in *ELT Journal*, but I am confident that *utiliser une langue approximative ou trop simple* can be avoided. "*Pensez boîte à outils!*" are the words my students have grown used to, and probably tired of. But whether they love or hate it, my trademark motto gives them pause. The ones who mobilize their tools, new and old, to get out of an impasse and move forward with accuracy are my stars — no matter how long they take.

C *Vous faites partie d'un jury de recrutement chargé de sélectionner le(la) candidat(e) le(la) plus compétent(e) pour un poste.* Step one: knowing what the position and its requirements are. Step two: collecting information on all applicants, their career paths and professional experience before, and this is step three, identifying their assets and flaws in relation to the job. The last step and actual task performance is the selection process when each student argues for their chosen candidate until consensus is reached.

L That makes sense. Getting back to the tool kit, what would it contain for step two, for instance?

C Without *le passé composé* and *les indicateurs temporels (depuis, pendant, il y a …)*, discussing a candidate's professional experience is nearly impossible, unless language accuracy is not part of the deal. A choppy "*Monsieur X est avocat pour quinze ans, depuis 2000 à 2015, puis il commence à enseigner le droit*" is understandable but not acceptable from a linguistic point of view. The correct sentence, "*Monsieur X a été avocat pendant quinze ans, de 2000 à 2015, puis il a commencé à enseigner le droit,*" requires specific language taught for a specific purpose — in our case, past tense and time expressions to review and discuss applicants' resumes.

L Impressive. How about when students introduce language they didn't learn in class?

C If they make proper use of it, great … but rare — rarer still when

CLASSROOM DRAMA

C "I bet even the French cannot understand this!" would declare a resentful student each time we'd listen to audio texts. *"Oh que si!"* was my silent response, followed by a collected, "Once again, at this level, the goal is to gather the information you need to proceed with your task. The rest can — and probably will — remain a jumble of sounds. It is best you let go of it. Let's try again." A dissenting grumble would be heard next and not until the coveted pieces of information filtered through his ears was he able to relax.

No doubt *prêt-à-comprendre* materials would have made him happier. Custom-built to students' levels, they satisfy a need for safety and control, but pale in comparison to authentic sources: newspaper or magazine articles, emails and blogs, video clips, radio interviews, statistics, labels, menus, and more, provided they have "been produced for purposes other than to teach language," says linguist David Nunan.

Learners comfortable with the idea that grasping what matters is enough, plenty even — until they can grasp more, faster and better — are guaranteed a much smoother ride.

translation is the modus operandi. Not a good idea when even Google gets lost in it.

L How do you get them back on track when this happens?

C My advice is invariably the same: *"Pensez boîte à outils!* Use the tools inside your kit — and use them wisely." Making do with a limited amount of French requires some *souplesse d'esprit*.

L *Plus concrètement*, what do you mean?

C Back to the recruitment task. To express disagreement, a student might say: *"Je doute vous êtes correct. Monsieur X n'est pas un bon candidat pour le poste parce que ..."* Besides the vocabulary glitch — "to be right" is *avoir raison* not *être correct* — the first chunk is ungrammatical because ...

MURDER MYSTERY

L I would have given it a shot if I'd had access to the user-friendly guide for the audience that breaks down everything from the nature of the crimes being tried to the *principaux acteurs*. No worries about defending my opinions in a debate since they would have to remain private, especially if the accused had made headline news. "*Il n'est pas question ici de se prononcer sur l'innocence ou sur la culpabilité des personnes qui, un jour ou l'autre, ont été sous les feux de l'actualité.*"

Armed with all this info, I would gladly have been front and center at the 2018 trial of *la veuve noire*, the black widow of the French Riviera. Patricia Dagorn was accused of duping and sometimes doping a string of lonely elderly men. Convicted of two murders, Dagorn will have plenty of time to mull over her wrongdoings — twenty-two years, to be exact.

L … *douter* requires the subjunctive, which I don't suppose is part of the tool kit yet.

C Exactly. Although very diplomatic, "*Je doute que vous ayez raison*" is out of range at this level. Any suggestion for a more sober version?

L "*Je ne suis pas d'accord avec vous*" would be my instinctive go-to. Either that or simply, "*Non, ce n'est pas une bonne idée.*"

C *Par exemple.* "Less will do" is another of my class mantras until tool kits grow larger and "more" becomes a sustainable option.

L "Less will do" seems a reasonable strategy for the get-the-job-done French I used to help my kids thrive in their new language and culture. But how to manage the often unreasonable desire that came along later to take off into the stratosphere where complex ideas can be adequately, and even eloquently, expressed? A friend once suggested I observe a trial from the gallery routinely open to the public at Le Palais de Justice in Nice. I begged off, fearing that no amount of *savoir-faire* or *savoir-être* could prepare me for the theatrics of a courtroom *niçoise*.

C The spectacle of the real world is not to be missed, even when some of it eludes you. It teaches things that classroom learning can only approximate.

WHEN GRAMMAR STOLE THE SHOW

C Years ago, I was a language tour operator. I led grammar expeditions to the places of syntax and morphology, had a must-see list, and loved every bit of it. Touring must have pleased students as well — if subdued dedication is any measure of enjoyment. Their language skills developed through controlled practice, usually short, role-played situations. Multiple-choice exams measured knowledge, not competence. Road maps and matching tool kits? Not that I remember. *Savoir-faire?* Largely overlooked. And not the slightest mention of intercultural skills.

Things changed when task-based learning took center stage, and students along with it. The buzz of interactions replaced the quiet of guided tours, somewhat to my regret but not for long. I became a convert once my fellow teachers and I got our hands dirty. Curriculum revamping required us to think big and far: which tasks to create — personal, professional, and cultural — in order to map out gradual, coherent, and comprehensive language acquisition across levels. *L'ingénierie pédagogique* offers thrills as stimulating as grammar tours.

L So you do agree that role-play doesn't come close to real-life stuff.

C *Oui et non.* Because the purpose of the task and its context (when and where it takes place, who is involved, etc.) are simulated, students experience a situation that may, indeed, never be their own. However, when in the simulation, they are who they really are, follow their own thoughts, make their own choices, question, argue, explain, advise … behave how they would in real life should similar circumstances arise.

L And do they all go with the flow?

C Not the ones who swear by rules, examples, and drills, and yearn for control over the language. Multiple-choice or fill-in-the-blanks exercises fulfill that need; live interaction doesn't. To win the confidence of sticklers has been, and still is, hard work.

L I so get the joy that comes from having The Right Answer, even though it fades once you're slammed by situations that no

WHAT LOVE'S GOT TO DO WITH IT

L In a 2016 interview for *Les Lolos*, a blog written by a group of American expats living in Paris, journalist Lauren Collins, author of the memoir *When in French: Love in a Second Language*, shares insights about learning the language with Maggie Kim. Fluent at the time of the interview, Collins had only begun studying French in Geneva three years earlier.

"You reach a level where you can do the stuff you need to, maybe not with a great deal of flair and elegance, but then I think it's hard to bump yourself up to the next level."

She acknowledges that making progress is tough.

"It's hard to keep going once you've reached proficiency, once going to the grocery store isn't a problem. You need another event, a life catalyst to get you to the next level."

The interview ends with a mention of Collins's reading group at the American Library and her enthusiastic embrace of a volume of Proust's *In Search of Lost Time*. How exactly did this journalist immersed in professional demands and caring for her French husband and child advance to her current level of expertise? My imaginary version of the road map lands her at an intersection where task-based and piecemeal learning meet and greet. Francophiles wanting to find out more about the acquisition of a second language — and a second self — should read her engaging memoir, if they haven't already. Spoiler alert: her conjugations are coming along.

fill-in-the-blank can prepare you for. How about you? Have you been thoroughly transformed into a task-based devotee since our meetings at The Carlyle? Back in the day you seemed as taken with grammar as we were.

C That Claire wasn't a fraud, and the glitter of grammar hasn't faded since. But today, with a "formal" teaching hat on, goals to reach, and a ticking clock, I think task first — for pedagogical and personal reasons. I'm a natural "tasker" when it comes to my own learning experience as an adult.

I grew wings in May 2005 when a student and member of the team in charge of UNICEF's flagship publication, *The State of the World's Children* annual report, approached me to write and illustrate a children's story for the launch of the 2006 issue, "Excluded and Invisible.""La valse aux trois amis," retitled "Lucie et le monde des enfants invisibles," was published on the SOWC website the following December. How did I pull that off? A good eye, imagination, and hard work, yes; artists in the family, also true; but most of all, incentive. A children's story was my kind of task — one that involves language, design, and creativity. Precisely what keeps me going with our current project. Not a chance I'd be polishing my English as vigorously as I do writing these pages without Motivation *avec un grand M*.

L   Your commitment to task-based learning is an inspiration. It's also a wake-up call. I can't be a crack task-based student without a goal, but defining my goal lately has been elusive.

Do I actually want to write French prose like a native? Next question. OK then, how about a flawless business letter, with its stylized salutation and elaborate closing? Lovely, but I can't imagine what that business would be. I try to picture myself with a corporate meeting to attend and a briefcase, but that image dissolves as I flash on the moment when I learned that the *serviette* on the ground in a Marguerite Duras novel wasn't a napkin after all, but a briefcase. The minor drama of discovery reshaped my reading of the scene and my memory of the moment. Try expressing that rush of experience to those who don't get their thrills from language *découvertes*.

C   Confusion gives way to curiosity — amused curiosity. I have witnessed enough of your rushes to attest to this.

L   Exhausting, isn't it? The desire to feel that excitement again reminds me of my appetite for French, the thing I most fear losing. Satisfying that appetite makes me a nuisance in a crowded grocery store as I read ingredients listed in French of products I don't wind up buying, or when I eavesdrop on children chattering about their day at the nearby Lycée Français. I wouldn't want me as a student in their French class, off again on some weird tangent triggered by a footnote, yet that same impulse means there's a chance I may learn some small new thing about the language I love every day. I would argue that protecting and sustaining that appetite qualifies as a goal.

C   Anything that fosters engagement with learning qualifies as a goal —
more so in your situation, without France to keep the language alive.
When did you become aware that the "rush of experience" bears more
results than a class you might take — or a workbook you might pore
over on your own?

L   During a walk with my husband as we dodged potholes near our
home. Ours is a dark street and the lack of streetlamps no longer feels
charmingly pastoral. I was grousing over this and other things, among
them my inability to stick with a more conventional way of studying
language than my own piecemeal approach. By the time we got home
the consensus was that I was actually pretty happy doing exactly what
I'd been doing for years.

C   I had not heard of the "piecemeal approach" before. Are you the
first to think up the term?

L   No. A quick Internet search turned up an abstract published by
three researchers at the Laboratory for Computer Science at MIT. The
study, full of graphs and algorithms, addresses the problem of how a
learner — for example, a security guard robot, a taxi driver, or a trail
guide — masters an unknown environment. They argue that learning a
grid is better conducted in small increments rather than in a superhero's
single bound. A rookie cab driver, for example, would be advised to
approach his or her new routes using piecemeal learning rather than
trying to achieve mastery of city streets *d'un seul coup*.

My husband and I heard of this firsthand from a London cabbie several
years ago. Proud of his hard-won expertise, our driver regaled us with
grisly tales of "The Knowledge," the exam he needed to pass before
he could be licensed to drive a cab in a city notorious for its jumbled
geography of lanes, squares, mews, and roundabouts. Though we knew
nothing of the MIT study then, common sense suggested that little by
little, piece by piece, was the only way our driver could have mastered
The Knowledge and won his Green Badge.

C   Common sense, indeed. Now tell me, what happens when the
security guard robot butts up against an obstacle not once, but twice?

ERRANCE

L What more can be said about the crazy deviations from the grid that give me so much pleasure?

I first came across *Lire* magazine at a ratty newsstand on Fourteenth Street when our French group had just begun meeting. I didn't know whether the others would be as transfixed as I was by the excerpt of a book by photographer and filmmaker Raymond Depardon, or whether I could express my fascination with the word *Errance*, the title of his book and a theme that unites his luminous work and life. Wandering, and Depardon's experience of the word, would be forever fixed in my mind and almost a destination in itself. Looking back now, that excerpt emphasizes the commonplace nature of discoveries that often pull me up short.

It isn't every day that you learn a new word (let alone a fairly esoteric one) at the gas pump. Hose in hand, I stared at a screen I'd never noticed before and discovered that "jejune" meant unsophisticated or naive. What the screen didn't reveal was the third definition — lacking nutritive value — which brought me awfully close to *jeûner*, the French word for fasting. Learning later that *jejunus*, their common Latin root word, meant hungry was more precious than my tank of expensive gas. I would never think of the word *déjeuner*, *petit* or any other kind, in quite the same way.

The news and information network responsible for all this frenzy was GSTV, a digital media company offering its captive audience short broadcasts and loads of advertising. Would it be jejune of me to hope that in the future another word of the day with a French association might pop up? My mind wandered back to Raymond Depardon and one of his central ideas: "*C'est un peu ça l'idée de l'errance: qu'il n'y ait plus de moments privilégiés, d'instants décisifs, d'instants exceptionnels, mais plutôt une quotidienneté.*"

L In the cool clime of the MIT graph, our robot explorer calmly sizes up the obstacle, realizes it is the same one it bumped into before, and assesses its dimensions. No hysteria or self-recrimination. I like that explorer's MO. To distinguish a boulder from a pebble on the trail is something you can't do when "Houston, we have a problem"

FRANÇAIS AUTHENTIQUE

L Homeward bound after a trip to central California, I sampled an unexpected *délice* on my iPhone, a website for learning French called Français Authentique. The first of Johan's seven rules made me laugh: don't go to a French class. Clearly this explorer had moved off the grid altogether. No grammar lessons? No vocabulary lists? Johan had exquisite points to make about nontraditional language-learning, but the thing that impressed me the most was the appropriateness of his claim. He didn't promise that his acolytes would become fluent, however one defines the word. He did guarantee that learners at any level could *améliorer* their French, a vocabulary word that bears remembering.

By the time we got to Los Angeles, I had listened to all seven rules, even though Johan had advised us to undertake one a day. That kind of moderation would be a tough call for anyone today. The rich blend of blogs, podcasts, and videos Johan and his team currently offer is *un véritable artichaut* for hungry piecemeal learners tempted to gobble up the whole thing at once.

is the habitual response to any perceived obstruction in language — or in life.

How great would it be to assess the obstacle in French, whatever it is, then take an accurate account of its dimensions? Is the word, phrase, or tense central to the context and how many times have I stumbled upon it? Did it bring our conversation to a halt? Did misunderstanding it (or not knowing it at all) distort my understanding of an entire book or just a single passage?

C Great? Terrific! Your questions meet my definition of how to shine — on one's own. They belong to the independent learner's tool kit.

Piecemeal learning MIT-style and task-based learning (along with most methodologies, by the way) have another thing in common: step-by-step progress. The more complex a task, the more steps, each one building on the previous ones.

A HOTHOUSE OF LEARNING

C   As the bus driver parked in front of the motel, the sight of it shook me and my fellow travelers out of a lethargic spell. The place turned out to be what we feared it would, *un vrai cauchemar*: stained sheets, sprawling cockroaches, and broken door locks. I didn't bother checking whether the thick greenish surface outside my window was the swimming pool advertised in the brochure. Instead I found my way to the reception desk where much of the group had already gathered, resolved to leave on the spot. Here I was, miles outside of New Orleans with some forty French people on the verge of revolution and forty hotel rooms to find — and pay for — before nightfall.

That was August 1991 and the climax of my first summer in the United States. The lack of French-speaking guides had left a travel agency with no other choice but to hire me — a twenty-four-year-old looking for a summer job in New York, where the tour I was to lead would begin. The two weeks I had spent in the city the previous fall had stirred boundless enthusiasm, and not until we left for Philadelphia did I realize the challenge at hand: to talk about places where I had never before set foot. Enthusiasm turned to anxiety after a bold account of the Revolutionary War in old Philly and gave way to sheer panic as the bus toured the Capitol grounds in Washington, D.C. On our first night in the capital, I pleaded guilty of fraud, which was highly suspected by then. My goodwill soothed the angry travelers and a deal was made: I switched from guide to interpreter, entertainer, and tour manager.

The New Orleans episode brought one last piece of information into the open: I was traveling under my employer's wife's name, which, he had told me, saved the agency money, and once filled in on the motel crisis, asked that I use her credit card to pay for different accommodations. He would deal with the motel owner. One threatening phone call was all it took to have him book us decent rooms in downtown New Orleans the same day. The group was happy but concerned when I became Christina P. and, now a real fraud, forged her signature to pick up restaurant and hotel bills in the Big Easy. I had won widespread support when all ended well and was declared the group mascot during our farewell dinner in Miami.

My title crowned *savoir-apprendre* more than a debut career in tourism. This experience was my first as mediator between French and Americans, clients and company, and for someone new to the U.S., I showed decent intercultural skills.

L   That the piecemeal learning system exists is a comforting thought. But it's also methodical and that's where I must part ways with my explorer. He will get to his destination a lot faster than I will, since my route includes twists and turns aided and abetted by the Internet. To crisscross and double back with Post-its and Fisher Space Pens that write even when the writer is upside down is my way of creating my own French connection.

C   Would you agree to making "creating one's own French connection" our definition for autonomous learning?

L   Despite wild deviations from the grid?

C   Provided they keep you going. I would tire of chronic *grands écarts*, but your route is not mine, nor is it anyone else's.

L   And one is not better than the other. Think artichoke. Lots of leaves, lots of different ways to learn. 🪶

8

Book Basics
Le grand déballage

LINDA: Reading a novel in French can be intimidating for learners. And talking about literature in a satisfying way is often as challenging as studying the book itself. While I understand the function discussion guides have in generating conversation for book groups, their questions are rarely my own.

So how to exchange ideas about such a solitary pleasure? Claire and I decided to put our dialogue format on hold in this chapter and juxtapose our thoughts on teaching and learning via literature instead.

You go first, Claire, *et bon déballage!*

   C A recent squabble with my spell-checker ended with a surprise. The French word *cancre* (dunce) I meant to type as I drafted this chapter stubbornly changed to "cancer" each time I pressed the space bar — so stubbornly, in fact, that a search was in order. The two happen to stem from the same Latin root and word for "crab." An etymological tie Daniel Pennac often points out when interviewed about his autobiographical essay and best-selling phenomenon, *Chagrin d'école*. Like the crab, a dunce moves sideways instead of forward, unable to follow "the straight line of academic achievement." And once the dunce takes hold of you, it never quite lets go: "*il reste là, accroché comme un crabe,*" lasting reminder of those dreary zigzags.

Or so says Pennac. That this acclaimed author and amiable, eloquent, and lively speaker spent one entire year learning to write and read

LITERARY LARGESSE

L Let's say you've fallen hard and would like nothing better than to hear the author speak about that book you love in your own city. If the writer is already going to be on tour in the U.S., the Book Department at the Cultural Services of the French Embassy in New York could make it happen. The department will review your application and might actually pick up the tab for the airfare, so why not be bold and contact the French department of your local university to inquire about a possible collaboration?

And don't despair if your favorite author isn't scheduled for a tour. The French Embassy will consider your request anyway if you follow their guidelines for submission. *Bonne chance!*

le *A majuscule* — "*la fonction de la majuscule est d'ouvrir la porte de la phrase, donc la porte des périls orthographiques et grammaticaux,*" he explains — and still grapples with the inhibition that locked him in until his late teens is hard to believe. That he chose to devote his teaching skills to children with learning difficulties less so. A choice as admirable as his unlocking method is unique. *Chagrin d'école* moved and astonished me. To have teenagers who, first thing in class, claim *qu'ils s'en foutent*, reflect about the grammar of their statement and its pronoun *en* — *s'en foutre, certes, mais se foutre de quoi?* (to not give a fuck about what?) — sets the tone for the school year. And what a tone. Not only did Pennac's *je-m'en-foutistes* wind up learning classic literature by rote, they could recite it at the drop of a hat — his magician hat.

But if memorization is clearly not the dusty classroom ritual its critics (myself included) would dismiss it as, it is not, either, what pulled Pennac out of his *cancrerie*. A novel did: the novel his eleventh-grade French teacher, intrigued by the young man's fanciful reasons for not handing in homework, assigned him to write in exchange for clemency. The task (Pennac was to submit a chapter every week) gave birth to the writer — and, years later, to the cool, compassionate teacher resolved to haul his own *élèves* out of their shells. After all, what's not to like about *un prof* who declares *ne pas lire* an "inalienable right" of the reader?

"*Le qu'en-lira-t-on (ou les droits imprescriptibles du lecteur)*" is the fourth part of another of Pennac's well-known essays, *Comme un roman*, published in the early '90s. The pun of the title — echoing *le qu'en-dira-t-on*, a popular term for "what (bad things) people might say" — reflects Pennac's double endeavor at the time: to help the reluctant, disheartened reader build an appetite for books, and to do so with a clever *pied-de-nez* at the establishment. His disinhibiting list *dépoussière* the codes of conventional reading.

1. The right to not read

2. The right to skip pages

3. The right to not finish a book

4. The right to read it again

5. The right to read anything

6. The right to mistake a book for real life, also known as the right to escapism (*le droit au bovarysme*)

7. The right to read anywhere

8. The right to browse

9. The right to read out loud

10. The right to be quiet or the right to not defend your tastes (both interpretations can be found for *le droit de se taire*)

Now a staple in schools in France and abroad, the original list has grown longer, much longer, with pupils' own ideas for how to smooth the reading path. It has inspired me as well. No rights, just hints and tips intended for (but not only) the task-based reader.

"*Entrez ici, vous êtes ailleurs ...*" French indie booksellers launched their first national campaign with a fitting welcome. "*Flânez, partagez, découvrez, débattez ... Vous êtes dans une librairie indépendante!*" Bookstores are indeed places to wander, share, explore, and discuss —

ALBERTINE

C Any idea who — or what — Albertine might be?

1. The slice of the Antarctic pie claimed by the French.

2. The Sun King's favorite mistress.

3. New York's fanciest bookshop and salon.

Langue au chat, anyone?

1. Wrong, yet not far off the mark. La Terre Adélie, the only non-insular part of the French Southern and Antarctic Lands, was discovered by the French explorer Jules Dumont d'Urville and named after his wife, Adèle.

2. The sun dazzled you. There's no Albertine on the long list of Louis the Fourteenth's courtesans. Françoise d'Aubigné, better known as la Marquise de Maintenon, was the one sharing his bed most often — before and after she became his second wife.

3. Bravo. You must know your French classics. Albertine is shapely, elegant, and the talk of town, both in New York and in Paris.

and booksellers people eager to embark on a search with and for you. Don't miss your chance for an escorted book tour next time you're in France. *Parlez livres,* and consider this first task a success if you bring home a novel you can't put down. More, a *coup de maître* if your French book talk turns long distance. Your email to share feedback and thoughts will not go unanswered — just don't write it in English.

Not the traveling type? Not an expert in *savoir-être* either? Fine. Book talks in French are one click away, and given weekly by the authors themselves. France's cult literary TV show opens with a monologue — a famous someone thinking out loud, inspired by the topic of the week — before the curtain rises on François Busnel and his guests: a chosen few convened on the set of *La grande librairie* to discuss — sometimes weave — the threads that run through plots and characters. Please, settle in for a fine conversation on books you will want to read. Bernard Pivot has found his worthy successor.

Featured in each episode is an actual *librairie* and the top picks of its staff. *L'ovni littéraire? L'essai à lire d'urgence? La BD féministe?* The questions are fun, the *libraires'* answers widely heeded. I can only think of one who'd shy away from the spotlight and the definite article suits him well: *le libraire* is unique indeed, only to be found in the sweet and quirky eponymous novel by Régis de Sá Moreira. "*Poudoupoudoupoudou …*" Not him singing, but the doorbell announcing new, and often unusual, customers: the world's most beautiful woman; Death, its scythe in hand; the Dalai Lama in search of *Le Grand Livre de la Vie …* Even God comes in and out. No wonder: *le libraire refuse de "vendre de la merde."* There isn't, in his store, a single book that he hasn't read — and loved. And the love is mutual. "*Pour tout dire, lorsque le libraire lit un livre, il a le sentiment d'être aimé.*"

His response to literature leaves me questioning my own. How about stories I wish never ended? Characters now part of my life? If not love, then what is it? *Une belle rencontre*, without a doubt — the kind you need to make the most out of your French novel because only a book that you love and that returns your love makes literary language worth the trouble. At least with reading comes the option to stop and go back, as often and much as you wish. The question is, will you choose to, knowing what you're getting into? *Relire tout court* doesn't bring words, sentences, paragraphs you let float by at first read any closer. There is more, much more, to it than just "read again." I therefore suggest that *le droit de lire n'importe quoi*, number five on Pennac's list, be amended: "anything" should be a book you'll eagerly pick up again and again until dog-eared pages no longer point to roadblocks but moments of joy.

Easier said than done, agreed, but doable if "anything" is a book suited to your level. *Le dernier Goncourt* can wait. Meanwhile, though, do stay away from rewrites *en français facile*. Dumbing down comes with a price: a

A-LIST

C Some books make you feel loved; some even transform your life. I can't say any of these transformed mine, although they were declared the top twenty life-changing books by French readers. But who am I to complain? I didn't vote, and — confession — have only read half of them.

1. *Le petit prince* — Antoine de Saint-Exupéry

2. *L'étranger* — Albert Camus

3. *Voyage au bout de la nuit* — Louis-Ferdinand Céline

4. *L'écume des jours* — Boris Vian

5. *À la recherche du temps perdu* — Marcel Proust

6. *Le grand Meaulnes* — Alain-Fournier

7. *L'alchimiste* — Paulo Coelho

8. *Belle du Seigneur* — Albert Cohen

9. *Cent ans de solitude* — Gabriel García Márquez

10. *Les fleurs du mal* — Charles Baudelaire

11. *La peste* — Albert Camus

12. *Harry Potter* — J. K. Rowling

13. *1984* — George Orwell

14. *Le monde selon Garp* — John Irving

15. *Crime et châtiment* — Fyodor Dostoyevsky

16. *Le seigneur des anneaux* — J. R. R. Tolkien

17. *Le parfum* — Patrick Süskind

18. *Le journal d'Anne Frank* — Anne Frank

19. *Madame Bovary* — Gustave Flaubert

20. *Les misérables* — Victor Hugo

storyline going express, leaving characters voiceless and the scenery just a blur. The only rewrite I used for teaching purposes, *Le mystère de la chambre jaune*, did the job it was intended to do, to immerse students in the past tenses of French, engage them in the dialogue between *imparfait* and *passé*

TOUT ÇA POUR UN ROMAN!

Ⓒ Paris, Place Gaillon. 8 November 2010, shortly before 1 p.m. Who is this man, causing such a media stir?

And this one? Same address and time, on 3 November 2015.

And all the others who, each year since 1914 on an early November afternoon, have made a circus of the quiet Place Gaillon? Do not be fooled by the rock star treatment: these guys are writers. Yes, *"tout ça pour un roman!"* as a

baffled tourist exclaimed. But not just any novel, *cher monsieur*. A Goncourt Prize–winning novel.

Reigning over no fewer than two thousand literary awards, France's top prize was born out of dissent. Because he disagreed with the long-established Académie française and its taste for the classical, French writer and publisher Edmond de Goncourt funded the creation of the Société littéraire des Goncourt, later defiantly dubbed the Académie Goncourt. The *prix* honors *"l'originalité du talent, [les] tentatives nouvelles et hardies de la pensée et de la forme"* and is awarded every November at the restaurant Drouant. A dining table in the Salon Goncourt has, since 1914, served as the office of les Dix who discuss and deliberate while feasting on *haute cuisine*. Bernard Pivot summed it up well: *"Drouant réconcilie la littérature et l'estomac."*

composé, but *quel ennui!* Gaston Leroux's ingenuity in masterminding this locked-room riddle is the only thing saved from the original. Particularly missed is the absurd touch that gives his writing flair and appeal.

So I wonder, would Leroux rather be enjoyed in a foreign language than read in a French, and voice, not even close to his own? Most likely. In his

NOT SO SIMPLE PASSION

L   *"Cet été, j'ai regardé pour la première fois un film classé X à la télévision, sur Canal+."*

The introduction to Annie Ernaux's *Passion simple* is a whopper. It's summer and the author is watching pornography for the first time. How fitting that this information be delivered with a one-two punch of the *passé composé* and its implication that a definitive end to this experience will follow.

In the subsequent pages, Ernaux examines her affair with a married man at excruciatingly close range. The mysterious A., citizen of an unnamed foreign country, comes and goes with irregularity — time is never more compelling than when she knows he's on his way. Much of her experience is conducted in the imperfect tense as she examines the hours, and sometimes minutes, in which he is present in her mind, her apartment, or both. She removes her watch just before he gets there, knowing that at a certain point he will always glance at his and leave.

> *Quand j'allais dans la cuisine chercher des glaçons, je levais les yeux vers la pendule accrochée au-dessus de la porte, "plus que deux heures," "une heure," ou "dans une heure je serai là et il sera reparti." Je me demandais avec stupeur: "Où est le présent?"*

Where is the present? It's a ringing question, especially when Ernaux realizes that she no longer thinks of A. the instant she awakes. The complexity of this transition is captured in a footnote:

> *Je passe de l'imparfait, ce qui était, mais jusqu'à quand? — au présent — mais depuis quand? — faute d'une meilleure solution. Car je ne peux rendre compte de l'exacte transformation de ma passion pour A., jour après jour, seulement m'arrêter sur des images, isoler des signes d'une réalité dont la date d'apparition — comme en histoire générale — n'est pas définissable avec certitude.*

Ernaux wonders when it was that she moved from the imperfect to the present as she details her passion with jarring detachment. Is this a footnote or a grammar lesson *hors du commun*? I'd say both.

New York Times op-ed "Found in Translation," Michael Cunningham does justice to the trade — "not merely a job assigned to a translator expert in a foreign language, but a long, complex and even profound series of transformations that involve the writer and reader as well" — and explains where it "gets more difficult":

> [Words] have music ... Language in fiction is made up of equal parts meaning and music. The sentences should have rhythm and cadence, they should engage and delight the inner ear. Ideally, a sentence read aloud, in a foreign language, should still sound like something, even if the listener has no idea what it is he or she is being told.

Cunningham's take on language resonates with me, for music has helped herd wandering words back to the text where they belong. Reading aloud may not endow them with meaning but creates a sensual experience that ties them (and the reader) together. Please try it, listen to yourself read. Can you enjoy the music and not study the score? Are you engaged and delighted, enough so to set meaning aside? Not a crazy idea with a book that captures the ear as much as the heart. And a rather good one when such a book is written in two languages. Just imagine, page after page of words shedding light on each other while playing their own tunes. More than bridging the language gap, bilingual books make it sing.

Haruki Murakami went as far as to "[find] himself in translation,"

LES LITTÉRATURES FRANCOPHONES À VOTRE PORTÉE

C If you long for a smooth, enjoyable read that is neither a translation nor a rewrite, look no further than Mondes en VF, a small online book collection designed just for you. Founder Myriam Louviot has all kinds of readers in mind when she says: "*Osez la littérature.*" The divide between literary ambition and accessibility was bridged by a handful of writers who said yes to writing for a multilevel audience. Whether big names of contemporary fiction or newcomers to its world, French to the core or foreigners, they represent a variety of styles and cultures and write for readers with skills ranging from A1 to B2. *Une visite s'impose!*

writes Roland Kelts in the *New Yorker*. "He wrote the opening pages of his first novel … in English, then translated those pages into Japanese, he said, 'just to hear how they sounded.'" It seems likely that Fred Vargas would lend herself to the exercise. "*Le livre, ce n'est rien d'autre qu'un orchestre … Il y a un type qui dirige; … chaque personnage est une voix, un instrument …*" is the conclusion she came to while attending the rehearsals of the Orchestre national de France conducted by Leonard Bernstein.

"He would take the raw material and work it with the musicians. After a month, it was no longer the same music. *Eh bien, un livre, c'est pareil.*"

How the cast of eccentric characters that populate her stories makes an ensemble, and plays music so well together, is remarkable, as remarkable as the adventures they stumble into. The queen of *polar* knows no limits. She succeeds in entwining the French Revolution and a twenty-first century Icelandic *fait divers* in *Temps glaciaires* — not her best work, but one of the few she's agreed to talk about. Her reluctance to give interviews showed on the set of *La grande librairie*. What started off as a curt exchange, however, magically gave way to a long, forthright talk on the creative process.

"*Je cherche mes idées la nuit,*" Vargas tells us:

> Hundreds flow by. Some swiftly go to the trash, some, usually the worst, inexplicably remain even though I make myself clear, "No, not possible, away with you," but who shows up at breakfast the next day? "Get lost," I say, "I can't write a story about a tree that grows in one night or a town crier in modern-day Paris." The last crazy idea, some boorish crime that made the news in Iceland years ago, just wouldn't leave me alone when, as if this wasn't enough, out of the blue came Robespierre. "*Ah non, Maximilien, tu sors s'il te plaît! Attends, je te rappelle les faits, hein, c'est un roman policier, contemporain, donc s'il te plaît, tu t'en vas, je ne peux rien faire de toi.*" Well, not easy when Robespierre insists. And sure enough, he stayed. "Fine," I told them, "but one of you must go, there's no way you two guys can fit in the same book." Robespierre did not leave, I expected no less

CULTIVER SON JARDIN

C By the look of her garden, my sister would not qualify as French. Tucked in a medieval courtyard, in the foothills of the Alsatian wine country, wildflowers and greens thrive and mix as they please — or so her artist's eye and green thumb make it seem.

With its poetic charm, her miniature garden looks nothing like *le jardin à la française* Le Nôtre made famous throughout seventeenth-century Europe. "The king of gardeners and Gardener to the King," who brought *l'art de corriger la nature* to perfection and asserted the triumph of order over "chaos," took Voltaire's acclaimed advice to a new level. Taking it to heart seems more reasonable. One should, without question, *cultiver son jardin* — while learning to see beauty *dans ses herbes folles.* That is my advice to gardeners of all ilks, bloggers included.

of him, and the Icelandic drama held its frozen ground, so I was left with no choice. *"Fred, faut que tu construises une histoire avec ça, l'enfer!"*

"Something rare just happened. Without my asking a single question, you told us about *le cœur de la création littéraire,*" concluded host François Busnel, evidently impressed.

I was too. Vargas's *déballage* thrilled and amused me. One thought arose unexpectedly as I listened to the interview again. I fancied she could inspire others — *vous peut-être* — to find their voice, a public voice, not on TV but somewhere public enough to spark interest. Why jot down reading notes on Post-its and scraps of paper or fill the pages of your beloved hardcovers with scribbles when you can fill blog pages instead? Your French blog, a space where thoughts on characters and plot, reading tips or troubles would be shared and discussed. A space to expand the world of books, tell fellow *lecteurs* about your search into the heart of French novels, and the gems you've found along the way. A kind of *Grande librairie* for self-made readers. All questions allowed and no fuss needed: book talk thrives on informal back-and-forth. How come *ne* is used without *pas* here, and why *de* instead of *des* there? Don't fret about asking — or answering. And remember, you can blush, sigh, and stare all you want behind your screen.

Now one more idea — and this one you'll love: if French gets in the way, switch to blogging in English. And don't be startled when, in the midst of work and fun, you experience what Vargas calls "the curious effect of language starting to move by itself." *Laissez-vous faire.* Let French surprise you: watch and listen to nouns calling for verbs, verbs for prepositions, prepositions for more … Language has a mind of its own; "[it] is ahead of us," she says, "and with it brings unexpected situations." Your French blog could well be one.

L Accommodating the group experience at Alliance Française de Los Angeles meant reining in my piecemeal learner *côté* somewhat. I worried that the details I enthused over would be too trifling to share or too narrowly focused on craft. We only had an hour and a half to talk books, as opposed to the unhurried two-hour-plus lunches in New York. Prepping for the discussion meant choosing a passage beforehand that I'd be called upon to read aloud and speak about coherently, a task-based exercise that, strangely enough, proved easier when a book didn't completely capture my heart.

I used to panic about getting through a novel in time for our meetings. If I burned through it too early, I wouldn't remember enough to contribute to the discussion. I tried blocking out daily page counts, a method that proved effective, but too mechanical. My anxiety subsided when I let myself read in French at whatever pace felt comfortable, lingering over demanding passages or zooming ahead to keep up with a fast-paced plot. This meant the occasional weekend doing little else. It also meant that I learned to stop flogging myself when neither method worked and I couldn't keep up with the reading that month.

I began rereading my favorite books to prepare for this chapter, but determining which ones these were wasn't always clear. Characters who continued to live long after their stories had ended wasn't the sole consideration. I've discovered a special section hidden inside my chaotic bookshelf. It contains my *livres de chevet*, books that have won a place on my figurative nightstand. How to discuss my tastes with the *libraire* Claire describes so well when I meet her one day? If books that are hard to categorize constitute a genre, I've already found my favorite aisle in the *grande librairie* of my imagination.

Trying to figure out the way a novel is built can mean going over a passage several times. Examining why a flashback or character revelation occurs where it does and what it does for the structure as a whole grounds me in the enterprise. What some might consider minutiae is often a big deal for me. The reading triggers questions about grammar and word choice. Much as I'd like to believe that exposure to proper spelling, for example, would eliminate my own *fautes d'orthographe,* I understand this is a fantasy. But puzzling over the writer's intentions and filling the margins with questions keeps me in the game and enlivens the experience. Books are both the work and the payoff for the work I've done to get here. Questions can be a tribute to the author. Taking the trouble to ask them means caring enough about the work to have had them at all.

How did so many books wind up on my shelves in the first place? I picked some of them myself, but mostly it was Claire, along with members of the French group, who did the choosing in New York.

OUTSIDE THE BOX

L   The massive heat wave in June of 2019 nearly curtailed plans to visit *La tête carée,* an improbable municipal structure I was determined to see. My hotel map was covered with ink stains from various shopkeepers who each suggested yet another conflicting route through Vieux Nice to avoid the blazing sun. *Sortir des sentiers battus* by following a trio of schoolgirls was one option when the map became incomprehensible. Luckily they had the same destination in mind.

It was worth the trek to stand in the shade of this sardonic monument, stare at the massive block of offices containing three floors of books solidly balanced on a chin, and consider the range of artist Sacha Sosno's possible messages.

DISAPPEARING ACT

L Lainé's dreary, unnamed village may or may not be considered part of the provincial France worlds away from Paris, but it got me thinking about *la France profonde* that figures enormously in the literary imagination. I wondered whether it has ceased to exist in reality after reading Adam Nossiter's disturbing piece in the *New York Times* in 2017. Nossiter mourns the disappearance of the grocery stores, *cafés*, and other small businesses that have historically been the heartbeat of town centers all over France. He focuses on Albi, but the bell also tolls for Arras, Calais, and other provincial villages, according to the government report supporting his observations. I understand the need for the *hypermarchés* with their free parking and wide-aisled abundance, but please, France, don't crush those *quincailleries* with their must-have gadgets and *brocantes* full of secondhand objects that have stories to tell. They're part of the landscape too.

Nadine has done the same in Los Angeles. Their decisions have both accommodated my *niveau* and challenged it. Finding out what initially drew me to my French favorites of the moment has made the endeavor seem less random. Sometimes there really are reasons that I picked certain novels to love — or that they picked me. I'm learning not to be embarrassed when the reasons seem facile.

Pascal Lainé won me over with his opening paragraph in *La dentellière*, the novel I mentioned earlier. I'm not crazy about beets, but the description of a *département* in northern France shaped like a *betterave* suggested a place I wanted to explore. There was nothing for tourists or even villagers to buy since the local factory had closed its doors. The story of a red-cheeked, inarticulate *personnage* named Pomme, abandoned by her father and raised by a woman whose casual prostitution is narrated in a cool and fairly clinical voice, quickly became my kind of mystery.

An elaborate vocabulary (to me, at least) conspicuously embellished plainly constructed sentences. Why was the student from a *château*-owning family so driven to possess a modest woman who worked in a hair salon, and what was it he really wanted to possess? If he was so frustrated by her quietude, why did it take so long for him to leave? Did her lack of eloquence mean she was withholding, simpleminded, or operating in a space that surpassed language? When the narration abruptly shifted from third to first person in the final section, it was time for a quick *dialogue à deux* with my favorite *interlocuteur*.

Although he hadn't read the book in French or English, my husband had seen the film based on it. (He never mentioned that he'd reviewed *The Lacemaker* years earlier.) When I reread my ragged copy of the novel, it was clear I remembered more about my feelings for Pomme than I did about Pomme herself. To what extent had I rewritten the character in my own head? OK, so she did wind up in a mental institution, but that didn't mean my husband had won the debate. How did we find ourselves arguing about class and the power of language? It doesn't really matter. Our back-and-forth gave us both a good workout. We decided to go another round to find out whether his version of her (passive-aggressive and disturbed) or mine (clever *gagnante* who has the last laugh) was more accurate after watching the film together.

PATIENCE

L Be sure to read or reread Rilke's *Letters to a Young Poet* when conducting your literary adventures, no matter your age.

You are so young, so much before all beginning, and I would like to beg you, dear Sir, as well as I can, to have patience with everything unresolved in your heart and try to love the questions themselves as if they were locked rooms or books written in a very foreign language.

Which is exactly what we did a few nights later. My husband's original sense of the film was confirmed and his reactions to each scene remained intact. I returned to the book for a third time, an invaluable if humbling exercise that reinforced the importance of questions and the value of teasing out ambiguities with conflicting answers. Why had Pomme been admitted to a mental hospital in the first place? *"Et puis un jour, environ quatre mois après le début du jeûne"* … my gas station revelations about jeûne were back big time. Pomme's fondness for sweets and the sound of those apples she crunched took on meaning that the words "eating disorder" never could. And what about that radical shift in narration? With only a few pages to go before the end of the novel the

PIZZA PUZZLE

L *Le mystère Henri Pick* by David Foenkinos won a special place on my bedside table before I'd so much as ordered the book. That a novel inspired by Pushkin and allegedly written in secret by the deceased owner of a pizza restaurant could cause such a flap among the French literati seemed more delicious than the putative author's *pizza Staline.* An aside on page eighty-eight meant I wasn't alone in taking books personally: "*Les auteurs peuvent écrire les histoires les plus farfelues ou les plus improbables, il se trouvera toujours des lecteurs pour leur dire: 'C'est incroyable, vous avez écrit ma vie!'*" I'm inching along, as I often do with books I don't want to end, though how can I read this slowly and still finish before the film adaptation featuring Fabrice Luchini airs on TV5Monde later this month? *Mystère.*

storytelling moves from a vaguely creepy third-person point of view to a warmer and more sympathetic first-person finale that produced some *virage.* Realizations piled up, enhanced by my having watched the film. Years later in the narrative the storyteller was no longer *le conservateur* gazing at and troubled by a portrait of Pomme; he had become a participant in his own life.

I could easily have overlooked *La liste de mes envies* if Nadine hadn't chosen it for the book group in LA. The setup seemed formulaic: A woman, Jocelyne, runs a notions shop and her husband of twenty-one years labors away at a Häagen-Dazs factory. Two children later, she has gained weight and decided her husband doesn't find her attractive. Then she buys a winning lottery ticket that produces a predictably seismic shift, just not the one the reader anticipates. Even then the plot sounded too easy. That ad man and author Grégoire Delacourt created such a psychologically complex world within the universe of buttons and bows was mildly irritating. His voice perfectly captured the intimacy of a *mercerie.* Slipping into multiple selves is the novelist's job, but I still wondered how he'd done it so convincingly. *La jalousie n'est pas jolie.* I wished I'd written this book myself.

I wound up taking the book personally for a number of reasons. I love lists and so does Jocelyne. My desires were banal next to hers, but then I didn't just win *le loto.* When she deserts her shop and

TAKING OWNERSHIP

L Make sure the books you read truly belong to you, even when you check them out of a library or borrow them from a friend. Take note of what others have said when you can, and only if you care to. You'll find abundant sweeping statements by critics down through the ages when you're holding a classic in your hands. Or maybe your book isn't widely known or universally loved. Say you're a party of one and you've fallen in love with a turn of phrase you can't wait to deploy in conversation. I'm all for keeping track of small epiphanies, too, and always mark up the books I value most with cryptic notes that may only have meaning for me. Margot was so smitten with *No et moi*, a novel our group in New York read about a gifted adolescent girl who befriends a homeless youth, that she made a collage to honor the book and the experience she had reading it. Whether it's a collage or a tattoo borrowed from Baudelaire, an intimate response to reading French is sure to enrich the experience.

provincial Arras at last, she is headed for a very different South of France than the one she habitually visited with her husband. It was as if Delacourt had retraced my own steps, some of them leading to a very ordinary beach across from the racetrack in Cagnes. And *le camping* at Villeneuve-Loubet? I'd spent hours in a *café* not far from there while my daughter took ballet lessons. What was I learning as I marked passages with stars and exclamation points? There are few definitions in the margins, so this wasn't about enhancing my vocabulary. It was about rethinking my own experience.

Years ago a French friend was working at a conference in Paris so Savannah and I spent the day with her daughter since we would be in the city at the same time. We visited shops and parks, crossed the Seine, and generally traipsed as far as our tired feet would take us. I steered the girls into a *café* for a *grenadine*. As far as I could tell, the people having a coffee or a *pastis* were not unlike the clientele in Villeneuve. Animated people spoke a French I understood easily and enjoyed. I liked speculating about lives so different from my own. This was not a shared sentiment. Taking a solemn look around, my friend's tween declared that her mother would never have taken her to a place like this.

LUNETTES CLASSIQUES

L   An image from one of Claire's wonderful teaching moments seems to be catching on. A reader might consider mentally slipping on a designated pair of *lunettes classiques* when approaching Stendhal or Proust. Just having them ready to pop on will help for literature the reader perceives, rightly or wrongly, to be too difficult, too far removed in time and space, too something. Those imaginary glasses remind us to pause and recalibrate for the work ahead. You can even take it one step further and find frames for those special glasses on the Internet that are as *intemporelles* as the masterpiece you're about to enjoy.

Delacourt's novel took me right back to my memories of that place and time. His characters would have felt at home in that *café*, though my friend's daughter did not. Her observation puzzled me for years. Was the service lousy or was she conscious of class differences in France in a way I could never be as an American? Or was I more aware than I remember, in that *café* and others, taking mental notes for my own writing as I waited for my daughter to finish her work at the *barre*? I'm not sure, but a novel that helps me unearth these possible associations gets my vote.

Any other reason why this book captured my heart? I flip to the lined pages at the end of the book meant for the reader to fill with his or her own list of desires. My only entry was "mastering French grammar."

A surprising number of classics have a permanent place on my bookshelf. Though they're not my *livres de chevet*, that they are present at all on that shelf speaks less to my own ambition than to the initiative of my teachers. Even with the impetus a discussion group offers, approaching work deeply embedded in the French literary canon can seem too arduous. Ever watch the scene in the movie *Wayne's World* where Dana Carvey and Mike Myers genuflect before Alice Cooper when he asks them to hang out? "We're not worthy," they say in unison. I know the feeling.

Reading *The Red and the Black* in English as a student many years ago was not a consuming experience. You'd think a person plunging into the work again as a much older adult would seriously bone up on the events of 1830, *mais non.* It's embarrassing to admit that I dared Stendhal's *Le rouge et le noir* again because of charming illustrations and short chapters introduced by citations. Learning that the author played fast and loose with their authenticity only added to their allure. I was smitten with tempestuous, tortured Julien. Whether he's wooing a married woman or joining the clergy in an effort to move up the ladder of French society, I rushed to finish the portrait of an intellectually hungry young hustler as breathlessly as I would have any contemporary page-turner. Historical inaccuracies hardly mattered compared to the truths Stendhal told about the human heart.

Proust inspires as much trepidation as reverence and the army of translators and scholars assembled around this author can be oppressive. Readers don't need a PhD in French literature to justify taking a stab at the celebrated author. Published in seven parts between 1913 and 1927, *À la recherche du temps perdu* is Proust's best-known work.

Would I have responded to the meaning and music Michael Cunningham refers to in his essay without a secret weapon? Uncertain. The earbuds I scorned for too long became my best ally while pursuing this celebrated author. Whether this was simply because they physically drowned out all the background noise, or because they created a more intimate experience is a matter of debate.

Choosing the right recording was key. It wasn't until I stumbled upon a benevolent website that provides audio recordings for the blind that I could relax enough to fall under Proust's spell. Listening to the melodic voice of Monique Vincens while I read balanced the complexities of Proust's style and helped with my own easily ignited frustrations. Undertaking his famously long sentences along with my charitable reader and a pair of steadfast earbuds kept me from freaking out.

This method carried me to the end of *Du côté de chez Swann.* What would it take to jump back in? The Brits, who broadcast a ten-hour audio rendition of the epic on Radio 4 during a long bank holiday weekend, may have had the right idea. Nosheen Iqbal refers to the experience alternately as "literary long listen" and "event radio" in

LUNETTES CLASSIQUES, SUITE ET FIN

C The "magic" reading glasses turned up in a conversation Linda and I had years ago, in the very early stages of our *dialogue à deux*. I miraculously found its transcription (we'd talk long-distance equipped with dictation software) in one of my many *Artichoke* files. The glasses were a response to the challenge posed by, *encore lui*, the subjunctive — pluperfect this time. Here is what I said then, and would still say today:

> The rare encounters the French have with the *subjonctif plus-que-parfait* mostly happen in novels nowadays. I don't remember ever learning or using it, but when I spot it, because spot it I can, some very smart glasses automatically "turn on" — the pair specially made for *un français littéraire très soutenu*. If grammar allows it, they show pluperfect subjunctives as pluperfect indicatives or past conditionals instead, because these I use every day.

A short excerpt from *Le rouge et le noir* should make the matter clearer — a juncture in the plot that Linda described as "the breathless moment when Julien finally dares to reach for Mme de Rênal's hand."

> *On s'assit enfin, madame de Rênal à côté de Julien, et madame Derville près de son amie. Préoccupé de ce qu'il allait tenter, Julien ne trouvait rien à dire. La conversation languissait. Serai-je aussi tremblant et malheureux au premier duel qui me viendra? se dit Julien, car il avait trop de méfiance et de lui et des autres, pour ne pas voir l'état de son âme. Dans sa mortelle angoisse, tous les dangers lui eussent semblé préférables.*

Mes lunettes classiques will read the last sentence as follows: "*Dans sa mortelle angoisse, tous les dangers lui auraient semblé préférables.*" Both versions are correct, Stendhal's is more literary, mine just plain usual. So, if "usual" is what you're after, put your own magic glasses on next time you're deep in a novel. Who knows what else they may conjure up.

a piece for *The Guardian*. Both sound tempting and I'm sorry to have missed it. Preparing for the real deal in French via an English adaptation would have helped me reenter Proust's world more easily.

The most satisfying moments for someone who is a hopelessly nonlinear thinker occur when unlikely books cross-pollinate. This taste for the unexpected association governs how I write, how I think about writing, and how I read. The more disparate these correlations are, the happier I am.

What could *À la recherche du temps perdu* possibly have in common with *La dentellière* other than my enthusiasm? One of my favorite experiences of Proustian time was *l'heure d'Eulalie*, a protracted moment each Sunday when Marcel's bedridden aunt waited for a visit from her friend after church. The hour of Eulalie remained uncertain to the histrionic Tante Léonie, whose sense of time was imbued by anticipation and fear of disappointment. What if her friend didn't show?

How chilling to flash on this scene near the end of Lainé's novel. Pomme's great love has severed their relationship and the narrator describes the more suitable partner she could otherwise have had and their wedding day. An afternoon lunch following the ceremony goes on too long. Most of the men are soused, their wives are desultory, and the kids know to follow at a distance, since it's *l'heure des torgnoles*, the moment when they could get smacked. All it takes is a little dancing for things to improve. The children breathe easier once *l'heure des baffes est passée.*

I like thinking about the attention two such disparate authors pay to time. The idiosyncratic pleasure it gives me is not the sort of thing I would raise my hand in a book group to go on about and I'm not even sure it makes sense to write about it here. But it does remind me to urge readers to appreciate anything that strikes them as peculiar, pronounced, or both. Honor whatever that is and give yourselves credit for some serious noticing. You're taking on a book in another language, for heaven's sake, and your questions and observations have legitimacy. Cultivate them to deepen your own experience of language and literature. And don't forget to dance to the music. ❧

9

Quiet Please
Moteur, ça tourne!

LINDA: **Do we really have to whisper during the movie?**

C   Not when you're in your own living room with a bunch of friends, which is where all the action is in this chapter.

L   My children's father learned to speak English, in part, by going to the same John Wayne movie over and over between college classes in the U.S. His experience has long been part of the family lore, but I never thought of his approach as methodology until we began writing our book. How much did he learn about vocabulary and pronunciation from that repetitive exercise? What could he infer from Wayne's body language when his understanding of spoken language failed? The advice the star gave to Michael Caine when the young actor first arrived in Hollywood may never make its way into immersion training for instructors, but it certainly explains Wayne's appeal to a resourceful foreign student: "Talk low, talk slow, and don't say too fucking much."

C   Our advice won't sound as cool, but satisfaction is guaranteed: "Talk as much as you like." In fact, I insist on it. Forget the popcorn, this is artichoke territory.

L   There's plenty to talk about in *Les saveurs du palais*. The story unfolds as the former chef for the president of France lands at a research station in the middle of Antarctica, where she will begin her new job cooking for a team of French scientists and workers. We only spend a moment at this bleak outpost before flashing back to Hortense Laborie

CLAIRE AND LINDA FILM SOCIETY

L   A *habitué* of French movies is likely up-to-date on the latest Palme d'Or from the Cannes Film Festival. With any luck, he might even agree with this year's selection. Let's say his local theater also features older classics and devotes a week to the films of Marcel Pagnol, whose lyrical tributes to the South of France continue to captivate followers such as actor Daniel Auteuil, who created a series of remakes based on his films and books.

We'll also assume our film buff knows the area near Marseilles where Pagnol grew up. Friends will be eager for his insights after they've watched *La fille du puisatier* together. But twenty minutes into the 1940 version of the great old film things get complicated. Raimu's thick southern *patois*, so essential to his character, is harder and harder to understand and the film feels slower than he remembers. The enthusiast wonders what he ever saw in Pagnol.

Another learner decides to skip the movies for a change of pace and devotes an afternoon to streaming *Engrenages*, the French procedural series. So this is the policewoman her literature class couldn't stop talking about? By the second episode the rapid-fire French means she's losing words, then whole sentences, until her eyes drift down to the subtitles and stay there.

Both learners need to create a new scenario. During a weeklong French movie binge in LA, Claire and I alternately played writer, director, and member of the audience to transform our movies into a learning tool. All that's needed to do the same is Netflix or another streaming service. Want to think more critically about a film instead of simply liking or disliking it? Got a beef with the subtitles and want to write your own? We did too. Anyone patient enough to press rewind during tricky sections of *Tu seras mon fils* for a second or third time deserves congratulations.

How about an indie film that's just appeared in a local theater and is already on its way out of town? There's nothing stopping *une vraie accro* from seeing a new release twice in the same week. I did that for *L'atelier*, an unexpectedly moving film about a writer's workshop run by a Parisian novelist and the recalcitrant kids she teaches in the South of France. Notes that I scribbled in the darkened theater were illegible in the light of day, but the dialogue was slightly easier to understand the second time around. The French teenspeak was a tough code for this outsider to crack, but I did my best to listen and learn.

being summoned to the palace from her peaceable life in the country. Sound like a fairy tale? It is. But one based on the true story of Danièle Mazet-Delpeuch and François Mitterrand that provides an *entrée* into manners and morals at the Élysée Palace, via cuisine.

C   We get to sample *savoir-être* early in the movie — though running through the streets of Paris *en tablier de cuisine* is not it.

No such thing as cheesecloth in the fancy Élysée kitchen, which is why, in the midst of the elaborate lunch prep on her first day as the president's private chef, Hortense rushes to her hotel room. The precious fabric she always packs in her suitcase is a must-have when making her *chou farci au saumon d'Écosse*. Just before hurrying back, she calls the kitchen aide in charge of the Saint-Honoré *crème mémé* — sharing baking tips with

PADSYNTAX

C   Blame it on syntax if the protagonists of *L'élégance du hérisson* — who stole the show in the chapter on grammar — make an appearance yet again.

In accepting M. Ozu's invitation to dinner, Renée subjects herself to a number of transformations — new hairdo, new dress and heels — yet nothing quite prepares her for Mozart's *Requiem* blaring when she flushes her host's toilet.

"Confutatis maledictis, Flammis acribus addictis ... !"

This must, she thinks, be her punishment for self-adornment. The ensuing panic thwarts frantic attempts to unlock the door, and not until Ozu comes to the rescue is she able to escape the madness.

"Je ... Je ... Enfin ... Vous savez, le Requiem?*"* is all she can say once released. Her stammering explanation triggers inner thoughts of regret: *"J'aurais dû appeler mon chat Padsyntax"* — i.e., lacking in coherence. Her cat's actual name — Leon, in homage to Tolstoy — was the first in a series of hints that would give her suitor reasons to believe she is not *la concierge* she pretends to be.

poise and perfect syntax while sitting on the edge of her hotel bed, breathless, the phone in one hand and the cheesecloth in the other.

"Nicolas, quand vous ajoutez les œufs battus en neige, veillez à ce que la sauce soit bien chaude pour qu'elle les cuise un petit peu, voyez?"

This, I believe, is Hortense Laborie in a nutshell: a *grande dame* of cuisine and language.

L   Can you please explain what you mean by perfect syntax? One dictionary definition calls it "the arrangement of words and phrases to create well-formed sentences," which to me suggests a written exercise, yet you're referring to Hortense's delivery. On the Îles Crozet she interacts with a variety of young researchers and workers. How's their syntax and does Hortense's shift during their exchanges?

C   Your definition meets mine, but our takes on "well-formed" may differ. What it means here, I think, is "orderly" or "consistent," and in that sense, well-formed sentences can be spoken as much as written. Elaborate ones, on the other hand, tend to be written more than spoken — although, as shown by Hortense's speaking skills, that is a very broad generalization. She could well have said: *"Nicolas, attention. La sauce doit être bien chaude quand vous ajoutez les œufs battus en neige, comme ça, elle les cuira un petit peu, voyez?"* Her instruction would have been as clear — and, from a syntactic point of view, as accurate, only less complex.

Her eloquence — better than "perfect syntax"— is compelling, and quite so considering her coworkers and their way with language: a macho bunch in the *cuisine centrale* — the only comment her *chou farci* inspires is a scornful, *"Le chou, ça va faire pisser le Président!"* — then wild geeks on the Îles Crozet. There's nothing "ungrammatical" about the researchers' colloquial French. Now, was Hortense's roughened by months in the company of hirsute guys on a bleak island? Maybe. Still, they had better not have made *fautes de français* or else *c'était corvée de plonge,* she had them do the dishes.

Clear enunciation, a trait she shares with the president, is paramount to her poise. Would you say their French is easier on your ears? Did you learn from it, and if yes, what and how?

L The elocution of Hortense and the president was a pleasure. Not only was it easy to follow, it was tempting to imitate. I've repeated that line about the eggs several times to inhabit a level of French that's purely aspirational. Slowing down to sample Hortense's delivery was a great way to let the subjunctive soak in. Switching to your more relaxed alternative was fun, too, like sampling a linguistic *amuse-bouche* (or *amuse-gueule* depending on your *registre*) before sitting down to the main course.

TIDBITS

L Not to be confused with an *hors d'oeuvre*, an *amuse-bouche* is a tidbit occasionally served in a restaurant. Think of it as a gift from the chef designed to keep your mouth entertained before the first course. Its counterpart is the more informal (and some would say vulgar) *amuse-gueule* served at home.

By contrast, the syntax of all those bureaucrats tearing across the courtyard of the Élysée and reeling off terse instructions about where Hortense should and should not enter, or reprimanding her for the cost of her meals, sounded as inflexible as the message itself. Doubtless their French was very correct, but it wasn't a delivery I found appealing. Would a more relaxed syntax hold them back in that hierarchical world?

C Only if "more relaxed" was their one and only option — which of course is not the case. Politicians master the widest range of *registres*. What is said in the *couloirs* must, at times, sound so relaxed it couldn't be further removed from the impeccable formal French, oral and written, *de rigueur* in a *palais*.

The unappealing delivery might have more to do with pronunciation than with syntax, as is suggested by your adjective choice — "inflexible" — reminiscent of the Long Island lockjaw accent you referred to a few chapters ago. In fact, I wonder whether Hortense and the president's diction, so contrasting with the rest of the cast's, is a mere coincidence or the director's wish to have them savor words as they would black truffle fresh from Périgord.

Another contrast worth highlighting is that between Hortense's and the Élysée head chef's use of *tu* and *vous*. Never does Hortense cross the *tu* line with Nicolas, her much younger assistant. Because of their marked difference in age and rank, she could well have done so from the beginning and certainly when their relationship becomes one of mutual — and cheerful — partnership. Instead, she sticks to a warm, courteous *vous* all along, while her rival routinely uses *tu* for anyone he deems below him. And when he refuses to store a tray of oysters that only the large *cuisine centrale* fridge could accommodate, Hortense's *vous* has far more power than her wished-for punch in the face: "*Si je n'étais pas une femme, je vous aurais déjà mis mon poing dans la gueule.*"

L   As the relationship between Hortense and Monsieur le Président deepens, egos are bruised in the kitchen and she inherits the nickname for Louis XV's mistress, which she leverages for effect. "*La du Barry vous emmerde.*" As much as I would enjoy sounding this elegant when miffed, another exercise might be more realistic. How about if I applied Hortense's habit of talking to herself as I chop, dice, and *sauté*? Any chance this might improve my cooking, my French, or both?

C   Cooking *à voix haute*? Food tastes better when made in French! But there's no need to master our *cuisinière*'s copious repertoire unless

DICTONS GRAND-MÈRE AND MORE

L   *Les carnets de Julie*, a delightful show about regional cooking, is armchair tourism at its best. Playful host Julie Andrieu takes us to picture-book destinations in both city centers and provincial locations all over France in a temperamental vintage convertible nicknamed Micheline. Who wouldn't want to ride shotgun with this dynamo and let her worry about any mechanical hiccups along the way?

Spending an hour with Julie and her guests is one way to accumulate recipes, sharpen culinary skills, and see the countryside. It's no big deal if you're pressed for time. A few minutes on YouTube can be all a viewer needs for some banter about olive oil versus peanut for a *tourte de blettes, une spécialité niçoise,* along with a proverb that dates back to the fifteenth century. No subtitles may mean pushing rewind a time or two, but so what? *On n'a rien sans rien,* as Andrieu's grandmother used to say.

you want to follow in her footsteps. Start easy: you may read aloud from recipes first or get the hang of it with Laurent Mariotte and his two-minute cooking shows. And how about cooking-out-loud parties with fellow learners?

L Two minutes is all it takes to get hooked on Mariotte and *cuisine facile*. His fondness for alliteration works for me, and so does the one-question quiz at the end that might get me 200,000 euros in what I suppose is a kind of lotto. Who would guess a mackerel could be *titillé* with a splash of cider? That's a vocabulary word with staying power, since I'm apt to remember an odd image and there's nothing odder than tickling a mackerel. I don't mind looking crazy when I talk to myself out loud in French. I might even throw in a proverb or two from Julie Andrieu, a very different food celebrity.

Terrific idea about the French cooking parties with friends. How about suggesting they drop by to watch an episode or two of Julie or Mariotte to track appetizing vocabulary words? One of the goals, besides preparing and enjoying a great meal, might be to put those words to practical use while cooking, like spices you need to use before they grow stale. On another night, ambitious guests might tackle Escoffier or honor Édouard Nignon, as did le Président, and throw a dinner party in the style of *Les saveurs du palais*. If that sounds too ornate, maybe prepare a few *spécialités régionales*. Compare and contrast the linguistic mannerisms of Julie and her friends in Nice, le Président, and Hortense while savoring *une tourte de blettes*.

C *"J'aime bien quand les choses viennent de quelque part,"* says Hortense when deciding on her first dish as presidential chef: *chou farci au saumon d'Écosse et carottes du Val de Loire*. Both she and the president swear by their grandmothers' *cuisine de terroir*. Names of regions, cities, forests, rivers, and more permeate menus and conversations. So why not expand on your *spécialités régionales* idea? Members of your French Cook Club could take turns hosting dinner each month with one rule to follow: design a menu highlighting a specific region, its food and wine. The host would share recipes, the guests information and stories about the *région à l'honneur*.

I have one final question for you. We have a *palais*, a queen, and a king — for our lady is not just a local farmer slash self-trained cook

CHEF'S TABLE FRANCE

C   Fun on the best days, annoying on the worst: if growing up with my last name had its ups and downs, no doubt Alexandre Couillon has had his own share of patronymic adventures — only his ups have never been higher. Today the chef's notoriety no longer stops at the restaurant door where his name hangs. By winning over foodies from around the world, *le cuisinier de l'année 2017* also won a semantic battle. "*Aujourd'hui Couillon signifie intelligent,*" says renowned food critic Gilles Pudlowski.

In the opening scene of *Chef's Table France* season three episode two, Couillon opens and smells each one of the giant scallops that were just delivered. Not one passes his quality check — a verdict soon relayed to the provider: "*Vos Saint-Jacques, c'est de la merde.*" Couillon is a man of few — often blunt — words whose candor makes up for his lack of eloquence. When asked for advice on how to create a dish, he answers: "*C'est simple, tu vas sur un rocher, tu regardes devant, et tu réfléchis.*" At the ends of the earth, a rock with a view may well be all one needs for inspiration.

"*Notre cuisine, c'est l'île, l'île de Noirmoutier.*" The chef's philosophy and cuisine aspire to capture the essence of his remote island on the plate, its stories — and its wounds. Named after the notorious tanker, *l'huître noire* Erika, an oyster poached in a squid-ink broth, evokes the 1999 oil spill that disfigured the coasts of Brittany and ruined its economy. His restaurant La Marine's signature dish made food critic Laurent Vanparys cry — tears of sheer bliss.

> *Je vois encore l'assiette arriver devant moi, blanche, immaculée, et cet espèce de chose sans vraiment de forme, noire, et je me dis "mais qu'est-ce que c'est que ça?" Je coupe, je mets en bouche … J'essuie mes larmes, j'appelle Céline et je dis "on peut en avoir une deuxième?"*

Couillon may have won my heart — the ungrateful last name and the memory of summers in Noirmoutier (is it where I learned to swim?) play a part in this — but I have great admiration for the four chefs featured in *Chef's Table France.* Their cuisine involves much more than talent and grit. It shows a profound connection to nature and art. "One of the through lines from these episodes is how close each of the chefs are to their farms or gardens, both physically and philosophically," writes food columnist Joshua David Stein. As true as Sophie Gilbert's observation: "Most great art, after all, exists to appeal to a single sense. But food works to entice all five: sight, hearing, smell, touch, taste."

LES FEMMES DU 6E ÉTAGE

L The movie opens with a sweeping shot of rooftops that is bound to quicken the pulse of anyone who loves Paris. What traveler hasn't speculated about the apartments tucked under the roofs of those stately buildings? Fabrice Luchini stars as Jean-Louis Joubert, a prosperous third-generation stockbroker who has never lived anywhere but his spacious apartment, though he hasn't visited the sixth floor of his building since he was a boy. When his long-standing housekeeper quits after falling out with his wife, a striving and insecure woman from the provinces played by Sandrine Kiberlain, his genteel world is thrown into chaos. Joubert shortly becomes smitten with her beautiful Spanish replacement, Maria, played by Natalia Verbeke. He helps her carry a piece of furniture to her living quarters on the sixth floor, discovering the squalid living conditions shared by an army of Spanish housekeepers employed by other residents in the building. *Les chambres de bonnes* with no electricity or running water seem dubious territory for a fairy tale, yet we can hardly believe otherwise when Joubert later flings open the door of his Citroën and invites the ladies of the sixth floor to step into his *carrosse* for a picnic in the country. Driven from their own country by Franco's still repressive regime twenty-five years after the Spanish Civil War, Maria and her fellow workers offer viewers a serious slice of history recast with comedy and verve.

by the time she is mysteriously plucked from her native Périgord and sent to Paris: her culinary and farming accomplishments earned her the nickname Queen of Foie Gras and title of Chevalier du Mérite Agricole, the French agricultural industry's highest honor. So, a regal duo, fairy grandmothers, nasty cooks, and bureaucratic creeps — yet no magic ending. Would you still say the movie is a *conte de fée*?

L In the sense of it being a fantasy, yes. I find that magical quality even more pronounced in our next movie, *Les femmes du 6ᵉ étage*, where the rules of conduct in a staid Parisian home are radically overturned.

Whatever we call it, '60s period piece, comedy of manners, or fairy tale, there's plenty to discover about class and politics here. When Monsieur asks for, and receives, breakfast from the new housekeeper, each syllable is as perfectly presented as his egg. The stuffy furnishings hearkening back to the days when his grandfather lived in the same apartment combined with Luchini's meticulous speech and affect remind me that there is more to understand about French class structure. In the nineteenth century there was the landed aristocracy and the poor who worked their land, right? In the big fat middle were the merchants and businesspeople who tended to commerce. How do Luchini's character and his prosperous mid-twentieth century family fit into this picture?

C   The big fat middle was home to the *bourgeois*, resented by the poor and looked down upon by nobility — who would (and need) not dirty their hands with moneymaking. By the 1960s, the *bourgeoisie* were still big, fat, and busy making money in roles ranging from shopkeepers to bankers. Jean-Louis Joubert was born in the *bourgeois* upper class where his provincial wife strived to belong. Exhausted by a visit to her dressmaker or a game of bridge, she embodies the snob who exhibits a taste for wealth but lacks the artless refinement of the *crème de la crème*.

LES BOBOS

C   Since *New York Times* essayist David Brooks published *Bobos in Paradise* in 2000, the term has become widely popular in France, not to say overused. In her review of the book, Melinda Wittstock summarizes Brooks's take on "Bobos," the phrase he "coined to describe the new cultural and corporate hegemony of his cosmopolitan, computer-savvy contemporaries," as follows: "'Bourgeois bohemians' are the new 'enlightened *élite*' of the information age. ... They have forged a new social ethos from a logic-defying fusion of 1960s counter-culture and 1980s entrepreneurial materialism." The French see them, perhaps simplistically, as bourgeois lefties or *gauche caviar*, with "*le cœur à gauche, mais le portefeuille à droite*." And that kind of left is courted by many. "*Les bobos plutôt que les prolos*" was how the newspaper *Le Parisien* summed up former President Hollande's attempt at winning over the urban middle class.

Now to the point. *Les femmes du 6ᵉ étage* is the kind of feel-good movie a non-native speaker can enjoy watching without subtitles or pressing rewind — the first time around. The plot and language are easy to follow, and the maids' uninhibited Frespañol should help anyone relax about their subjunctive. But the movie has its share of quaint corners and I'm curious to know how you went about figuring out the old-fashioned idioms.

L   Watching those women navigate French with so much spirit and confidence was a reminder of the inroads you can make without perfect command of the language. They weren't impeccable speakers, but it didn't slow them down. In fact, reviewer Kenneth Turan noted that not all of the Spanish actresses spoke French and some learned their lines phonetically. Can you weigh in on how I tackled a few expressions I didn't understand?

C   *Je t'écoute.*

L   When Jean-Louis falls ill and the ladies hover over him with a terrifying-looking gruel to get him back on his feet, they exclaim that "*il est patrac.*" Not knowing what that meant didn't hang me up since their frenzied body language did so much talking. I wouldn't try to use *patrac* in conversation without knowing more, but I would recognize it if I heard it again, like someone you've met somewhere before whose name you can't quite place.

C   Great use of context! Now, what if you looked that "someone" up? A word you're able to hear and isolate from others — *une chance à saisir* given the twists and turns of French pronunciation — is a word you can learn everything about, spelling included. Most online dictionaries will do the trick. Just type in the first letters: p, a, t, r ... and the rest will follow: ... *aque!*

L   Early in the film the Jouberts' longtime *domestique bretonne* Germaine and her employer Suzanne explode at each other. Who will govern the household now that Jean-Louis's mother is dead, the daughter-in-law or the maid? When Suzanne steps over the line in an angry confrontation with Germaine, her husband chides her with an expression that I misheard as "*vous passez les bords.*" *Passer* can mean to go and *bord* sounds like border. You see how I got there.

EXTRA, EXTRA, READ ALL ABOUT IT

L   The ways in which critical opinions about *Les femmes du 6ᵉ étage* diverged make me flash on Jean-Louis's evolution *vis-à-vis* newspapers. Initially we see our fussy hero at breakfast, neatly arranging his copy of *Les échos*, a paper dedicated to business and the economy. When he later buys a copy of *Le Figaro* on the street, the paper his wife reads while having her *petit déjeuner* in bed, we sense that change is in the air. Staunchly conservative and founded under Charles X, *Le Figaro* signals that Jean-Louis is at last becoming interested in the world beyond business and finance. The *coup de grâce* is his acceptance of *L'humanité* from the political incendiary played by Lola Dueñas, who hands out copies near the church she and the other housekeepers attend.

It's an interesting leap to imagine Luchini studying the reviews of the film in the U.S. Kenneth Turan, former film critic at the *Los Angeles Times*, is clearly a fan of French farce and enthusiastically characterizes the movie as such. The critic for the *Hollywood Reporter* describes the film as a "benign comedy" and begrudges the lack of seriousness with which it handles the atrocities of Franco's Spain. A review on the Rochester Labor Film Series website cites the film's director Philippe Le Guay's desire "to render homage" to the Spanish women who fled for France to become domestic workers in the mid-'60s, but finds that the fairy tale aspect of the film trivializes their plight. Jean-Louis is being anything but trivial, however, when he educates *les femmes* about the stock market, then steers them into some decent investments. Their collective financial transformation is further underscored when Le Guay shoots them reading *Les échos*.

C   I do, and you got very close; only you stopped too soon. Time to hone those detective skills: What is the French for "step over the line" or similar expressions? *Dépasser la limite.* Next: What does *dépasser* have in store in your trusty online dictionary, and could it sound close to *passer les bords*? OK then, is *dépasser les bornes* what Joubert actually says to his wife? Yes, and it is also sort of what I encourage you and our readers to do here: not to go too far but far enough to "play" with what you hear. Add a syllable, swap a vowel or consonant with another, explore your auditory memory ... The time is never wasted that is devoted to proactive learning.

THE REAL DEAL

L How much do Luchini's films correspond to his life? A lot, in some cases. Jean-Louis looks right at home in the hair salon scene when the ladies of the sixth floor gather to prepare for a wedding, and it's no wonder. Luchini, a former hairdresser and autodidact who left school at fourteen, is hardly a stranger to the world of women. As a spécialiste en brushing, he knows his stuff. Who else could wax poetic over giving a dépilation to actress Marlène Jobert? Spend an hour with him on On n'est pas couché to learn about this and more, specifically his production called Poésie?, an homage to Rimbaud, Baudelaire, Molière, Flaubert, and Labiche, among others.

For his point of view about the class system in France, all it takes is some exposure to his argot and attitude in one of his YouTube videos. An unapologetic member of the bourgeoisie, Luchini makes ribald fun of his own tribe as he strolls along the beach at Île de Ré. The merciless riffs add more texture to his performance in Les femmes and provoke more questions. How and whom does he study for his roles?

L One more and then I'm done. Jean-Louis is a man in love and sparks fly when he and his wife throw a big party for clients and colleagues. They have hired an extra server for the evening who has eyes for beautiful Maria. Joubert fires him and before storming off, the angry serviteur strikes back: "C'est chasse gardée." Letting the infinitive chasser settle in for a minute or two helped. Garder kind of worked with that word, too, when I thought of Maria as a prize the server wanted to keep for himself. Mostly I thought of the huge and terrifying chiens de garde that used to lunge at my daughter on our walks in France. This association is nutty, right?

C Dingue, oui, but it works. This is, after all, a vibrant example of "creating one's own French Connection," which we agreed was our definition for autonomous learning.

I'll continue with a suggestion, inspired by your aside on the film's reviews. The Claire and Linda Film Society has honored its word: you, reader, and your movie friends have had a lot to talk about. Would you be up for some writing this time, and to share your own review with fellow critics? Check out AlloCiné, le site référence du cinéma et des séries TV, and what your counterparts in France have to say about the film.

You'll be surprised by the quality of both language and content. Click on *Rédiger ma critique*, create your AlloCiné account, and have at it.

L Being dispassionate will be a challenge after scouring the Internet for info on the star.

I took Fabrice Luchini at his word in *On n'est pas couché* when he urged one of the journalists not to worry that his compliments were repetitive. "*Vous croyez qu'on est des gens blasés? Que vous ayez aimé mon spectacle me transporte de joie.*" Still, I wonder what would happen if I sent my original email, minus your edits in the version below. Would someone so passionate about the French language have honored the effort it took for a non-native to write it at all, or cringed and pushed delete?

Cher Fabrice Luchini,

Je vais peut-être "dépasser les bornes" comme vous l'avez dit à Germaine dans Les femmes du 6ᵉ étage, *mais comme je suis fanatique de vos films, je me permets de vous solliciter.*

Je suis américaine et j'habite à Los Angeles. J'aimerais savoir si vous êtes ouvert à la possibilité de présenter Poésie? *sur la côte ouest. Vous feriez des heureux! Le Théâtre Raymond Kabbaz présente des pièces en français et vous pourriez y monter la vôtre. En voici le lien. Je suis membre de l'Alliance Française de Los Angeles et suis sûre qu'elle serait ravie de soutenir un tel projet.*

J'ai vécu presque neuf ans en France et trouve dans la musique et l'éloquence de vos mots une littérature qui parfois dépassent mes propres bornes de compréhension, mais jamais d'admiration.

Cordialement,
Linda Phillips Ashour

C Remember our conversation on *savoir-faire* and *savoir-être*? I suggest you read the first pages of "Louder Than Words" again and seriously consider sending his agent the note — faults and all or not, your choice. In any case, the time for your *soirée cinéma* has

CEBRIFA

C   It took watching a few live interviews to adjust to, and delight in, the way Luchini plays with language. If you need practice with *les registres de langue*, and want to hear the full range of them, he is your guy. Interviewed about his movie *Gemma Bovary*, he goes from coarse to sublime in the same breath — from the erection stirred by the actress kneading bread dough, "*Quand elle pétrit le pain, les mecs vont l'avoir en l'air!,*" to Stendhal's definition of beauty: "*La beauté, disait Stendhal, c'est une promesse de bonheur.*"

Even *verlan* is part of his repertoire. Never before had I heard a star of Luchini's standing answer journalists in the popular slang. "*Une meuf à tomber dans les meupos*" is another description he gives of Gemma. Translation: *une femme à tomber dans les pommes*, literally a woman to faint for — exceptionally beautiful. *Verlan* is a code language originally used among criminals in which the syllables of standard French words are reversed or recombined, or both — *verlan* itself being a verlanization of *l'envers*, meaning "the reverse." In the mood for more? Please enjoy La Fontaine's fable "Le corbeau et le renard," recited by Luchini himself, who else?

come. The wealth of information you've gathered on your star and *Les femmes* must be shared — before, after, or even during the movie. Your guests will thank you for a richer, deeper experience. And be sure to expect a full house, because you will have done all the work. But the next one is on them.

My *soirée* would star Gilles Lellouche. Mind the spelling. He is not, as I thought he was, related to famous French director Claude Lelouch — although his directorial debut would entitle him to be. With ten nominations at the 2019 Césars, *Le grand bain* made a splash. It was, by chance, one of the three Lellouche movies playing on a recent flight back to New York. Binge-watching? Not when each took me to a different planet, confirming the actor's reputation as a *comédien caméléon*. You and I loved him in the role of Bruno, the good-hearted drug lord in *Ne le dis à personne*. The thriller is based on *Tell No One*, a novel by Harlan Coben, American master of suspense. Would you say the movie is more French or more American?

L   In principle we could be anywhere when the movie opens, except that we're not. Language aside, there's no question that this is a French film in that first anchoring dinner party scene outside a ramshackle country house. The bottle of *pastis*, the cigarettes, and a baby at this table of *bon vivants* suggest that this is no backyard barbecue. All the more surprising, then, that individual moments made me flash on America, seamless as the book-to-film adaptation was.

We don't stay at that gathering of friends for long. Later in the film when things have taken a dark turn, Dr. Alexandre Beck gives his pursuers the slip by running across *le périphérique* near the hospital where he works. The band of highway that separates Paris proper from its *banlieues* is more than a geographical obstacle. It's also a psychological barrier suggesting many things, crime and *les immigrants* among them. It could be that I've been conditioned by too many action films, but visually the scene seemed quintessentially American. I went straight to Liam Neeson and a similar leap he made to save his kidnapped daughter in *Taken*. Learning that he was being courted for a remake of *Ne le dis à personne* was both surprising and no surprise at all.

C   Lellouche shares your opinion: the scene of *le périphérique* is classically American, although shot "*sans débauche d'effets spéciaux*" — and in that way French as well. "French people need to believe what they see. Movies are filmed in natural settings, so people can say, '*Ah je connais cette station de métro, je connais cette rue, c'est vraiment dans Paris.*'"

L   The drug dealer, who also happens to be Dr. Beck's personal savior, must have been a complicated tough guy to translate. In the book Beck puts out his hand for him to shake, but it's a no-go. "Tyrese ignored it and hugged me fiercely," Coben writes. A French friend recently went on at length about finally mastering the art of *ze* American hug after having lived in LA for years. A detail, I know, but one I'm sure the film's director considered.

C   Provided he or she has your eye for detail! Any others that spark cross-cultural thoughts?

L   After three screenings I'm not sure whether it's more French or American. The film flew by in a rush the first time. Watching it again (and again) helped me untangle the intricate plot and enriched the experience. I'd call it a cross-cultural hybrid, but my guests will need to weigh in on that one. I'm going to ask them to read *Tell No One* before our movie date. Coben's novel is a pleasure in its own right, but doubly so for proactive learners who want to compare the high-speed trips through Paris and suburban New Jersey.

One thing that the book couldn't help me with, though, was *argot*. If I had the energy, know-how, or both, I would create a down and dirty glossary of tough guy, hardened cop, and criminal slang. Since that's beyond my ken, I'm handing this one over to you, Claire. Was it just me, or was the language every bit as complex as the plot in this film?

C   I'd say typical of thrillers. I recently gave *The Usual Suspects* another shot, and would have missed half of the movie again without English subtitles, the *Dictionary of Slang and Unconventional English*, and the option to pause and rewind. A down and dirty glossary must be earned, *ma chère*. Let me know what you think of this one.

L   Definitely helpful. I'm printing this out for future reference.

C   You can put it to use this minute. Please read the sentences below (both lines from the movie) and tell me what they have in common — sociolinguistically speaking.

"*Mettez-ça sous vot'cul, vous allez m'pourrir la caisse. Vous avez foutu l'bordel sur le périph …*" (Bruno to Alexandre Beck.)

"*Qu'est-ce que j'en ai à foutre que ça fasse chier tout le monde! C'que j'veux, c'est la vérité.*" (The police inspector to his assistant.)

L   Could you first elaborate on the meaning of "sociolinguistically"?

C   Sociolinguistic skills are embedded in *savoir-être*. They refer in part to the ability to adapt language (word choice, but also intonation, etc.) to a specific audience and context. Greeting a person you're being

DOWN AND DIRTY GLOSSARY

C Some basics first.

- *(se faire) serrer: (se faire) arrêter*

- *chelou (verlan de louche): bizarre*

- *(se) planquer: (se) cacher*

- *balancer: dénoncer*

- *foncedé (verlan de l'argot défoncé): drogué*

- *beuh (contraction de beuhr, verlan de herbe): herbe, cannabis*

- *keuf (contraction de keufli, verlan de l'argot flic): policier*

- *vilci (verlan): policier en civil*

- *zonzon ou zonz', carpla (verlan de placard): prison*

Now the down and dirty type — but oh so common, and not only in *Ne le dis à personne*. So please, pardon my French.

- *merde, putain, con:* but of course, those you know

- *fous le camp!, casse-toi!, tire-toi!, dégage! (foutre le camp = se casser/tirer = dégager):* get the fuck out!, get lost!

- *tu te fous de ma gueule? (se foutre de la gueule de quelqu'un):* are you fucking kidding me?, are you fucking with me?

- *un(e) casse-couille:* a pain in the ass, a ballbuster

- *vous avez foutu le bordel (foutre le bordel):* you made a (fucking) mess

- *tu me fais chier, tu m'emmerdes (faire chier = emmerder):* you are pissing me off

- *(j'en ai) rien à foutre, je m'en bats les couilles (ne rien en avoir à foutre = s'en battre les couilles):* I don't give a damn/ shit/fuck

For more, go to Dictionnaires.com: *argot* is one of the forty sleek *glossaires spécialisés* offered in this collection.

introduced to at a formal event with a cheerful *Salut!* is a sociolinguistic or cultural *faux-pas* in France. Does that help?

L Got it. Some of these sentences challenge everything learners like me hold dear about the subjunctive, that supposed marker of elegant speech. "*Qu'est-ce que j'en ai à foutre que ça fasse chier tout le monde!*" There's nothing refined about the expression *faire chier*, as you've shown in your glossary, so what's the subjunctive doing here? Similarly, "*Mettez-ça sous vot'cul*" baffles at first glance. So you can suggest someone place something under one's ass and still use *votre*?

C I could indeed. And would if I spoke in Bruno's *registre* and thought Dr. Beck deserved a *vous*. Slang and social code aren't mutually exclusive. Neither are slang and the subjunctive, and that it carries elegance has proved a resilient misconception. In our chapter on grammar, you reminded me of my "corporeal demonstration" of the mood at The Carlyle. Well, "*Qu'est-ce que j'en ai à foutre que ...*" is expressing emotion, subjectivity — i.e., appreciating the reality *faire chier tout le monde* represents. That's what the subjunctive has to do with it. There are no better movies than thrillers to take the glitter off grammar.

L Having said all this, I'm still grappling with your initial question. While the *argot* in the film is French through and through, American lyrics and melodies express both themes and plot points in four separate tracks. What better ode to a romance rooted in childhood memories than Otis Redding's recording of "For Your Precious Love"? Jeff Buckley's "Lilac Wine" is an achingly beautiful accompaniment to Beck's state of mind in scenes that flip back and forth between his wedding and a funeral. "With or Without You" becomes a one-man anthem when Beck discovers a crucial message in a computer *café*. He instantly goes on the run, and "Hands of Time" goes with him. He can't turn back now and neither can we.

What would you think of reconfiguring these scenes substituting French music? At the very least, searching the Internet for rock and pop classics would expand any musical vocabulary, or even create a whole new one. I went to Radio.net and found RTL2, a station where I could test the waters and came across some frothy pop songs on a podcast called *Made in France*. I didn't turn up anything that would work for our film, but it was love at first listen. I may have to become a regular.

C Why not start there? A sampling of eclectic music will whet the appetite for more. Think *entremets*, think pleasure, then raise a glass to both.

L As long as we're offering a toast, let's close our discussion with *Tu seras mon fils*, a film that may change the way viewers think about French wine and *terroir* forever. It's not enough for vintner Paul de Marseul, played by Niels Arestrup, to crush grapes as he creates his fine wines. He must crush his son as well, displacing poor, stumbling Martin (Lorànt Deutsch) for Philippe (Nicolas Bridet), the son of his caretaker and business partner. This is a film with grand themes, lavish landscapes, and language to match. The translators had their work cut out for them. Remember tinkering with the idea of creating a "Worst Subtitles List," when we came across "jugged hare" for *civet de lapin*? *Les sous-titres* were of little help when it came to expressions like "*Tu me pompes l'air*" or "*Il ne se mouche pas du coude.*" He doesn't blow his nose with his elbow? Apparently not, if he's an aristocrat or a member of *la haute bourgeoisie*.

Another exercise I decided to skip was an amateur comparison of the *argot* in *Tu seras mon fils* with the *argot* in *Ne le dis à personne*. Instead I let myself sink into the luxuriant scenes on my last viewing, much as Paul and Philippe soaked in a bath of grapes in a Paris spa. Not being much of a wine drinker myself, I'm a little tone-deaf about the whole business. It took a drama about a domineering winegrower in search of a worthy successor to get my attention.

I wound up approaching *Tu seras mon fils* almost as a process film that could teach me *le béaba*, or basic knowledge, of the industry. I came away with new information and a lot more respect for *le terroir* and the very good life it can produce, down to the gleaming boots that Paul gives to Philippe when the older man enters the ranks of la Légion d'honneur. Did my passive viewing mean I was being lazy, or does watching a deeply atmospheric film in this way function as a valid learning technique?

C Your choice about how and what to learn says a lot about the independent, self-aware learner you have become. The Linda intent on getting it "just right" as this conversation began a long time ago welcomed back the adventurer of earlier years who embraced true immersion in France — and recreates it today with her piecemeal approach. You've opened a new door to learning — for yourself and others. And no doubt even a Grammar Girl would gleefully let herself "sink into the luxuriant scenes" of a movie.

Think of your split learning personality as a gift. The piecemeal and get-it-just-right you's are not competitors, they complement each other, feed on each other's practice. So be kind to both learners. *Promis?*

P.S.: Before your next soak, I recommend you get acquainted with the work of two artists: Matthieu Chedid, singer, songwriter, guitarist extraordinaire, better known by his stage name, M, who composed the original score for *Ne le dis à personne*, and Delphine de Vigan, cowriter of the script of *Tu seras mon fils*. Her novel *D'après une histoire vraie*, recipient of the 2015 Prix Goncourt des Lycéens, was my introduction to autofiction and one I will not forget. ❧

10

Here at Last
Bel et bien là

LINDA: What does a British game show have to do with piecemeal learning? A lot, if you ask me.

The game show is called *Only Connect* and the contestants' goal is to discover the common thread in apparently random things. The popular and spectacularly nerdy series takes its name from one of my favorite quotes by E.M. Forster: "Only connect! ... Live in fragments no longer."

I don't mind those fragments. In fact, they've become the snap, crackle, and pop that keep me going. What's better — and far more substantial than Rice Krispies — are moments when scraps of language, learning, and plain old living combine to create a larger whole.

Waiting for a passing train isn't all that exciting, until one day when it is. It was hot and I was selfishly annoyed by passengers who were moving a lot faster than me. I sat in my car, remembering Proust and an expression I'd flagged in the margins of *In Search of Lost Time*. "*Le train-train de la vie*" perfectly captured the chugging along that composes so much of life. Snap. Crackle. The pop came later when my daughter called that night, insisting that my husband and I watch a Quincy Jones documentary on Netflix, some of which had been filmed in France. His daughter, actress Rashida Jones, had produced the movie. And her production company is called Le Train Train. That Proust, Quincy, and Rashida had all come together meant my ordinary day was no longer ordinary. I had taken a quick trip to France in my mind.

Do moments like these constitute my heart of the artichoke, the maxim Claire and I set out to explore when we began writing this book? Yes. Even though my grammar and writing in French is still laughably what it is? Absolutely, although I couldn't have said this before coauthoring a book with Claire.

In our final chapter I mentioned a podcast called *Made in France*. What I didn't explain was why the song I first heard there, "À quoi ça sert," written by Axelle Red, was love at first listen. Here's a snippet, by the Belgian singer-songwriter and human rights activist:

Bien souvent je me demande

Le but de ces efforts

Le but de tout vouloir apprendre

De bouleverser mon sort

Je cours après la perfection

Mais je n' peux plus avancer

Non plus m'arrêter

À quoi ça sert

Ces sentiments profonds oh, non

Je me sens de travers

À force de voir mon monde à l'envers

Faut qu'je cesse de m'inventer des questions

Non

À quoi ça sert

Axelle continues, but she's given me all I need right here. So I'm not the only one who has a problem with perfection. She's not necessarily talking about the French language, but I am. Part of this striving comes with the territory. French is exacting. The trick for a learner, this one at least, is to lighten up on the inevitable mistakes and take pleasure wherever it can be found. Sometimes that can be in picking up a single new word. My latest is *tarabiscoté*, which is the fantastically French word for fussy. It's also emblematic of many of the *Lettres de Figaro* on language that turn up in my inbox. I almost never get a good score on the spelling tests and have usually committed most of the other grammatical errors that have the writers tearing their hair out. More and more that doesn't stop me from having a great time, learning a little something while I'm at it, and feeding the beast that requires some care and nurture.

I do have one question that's both piecemeal and task-based in nature. Since I haven't the patience/fortitude for the grammar drills calling my name, am I getting any better at this enterprise called French? In the beginning I saw ours as a hopeful book, but what can the reader hope for after having finished it?

I got a partial answer from a recent visit to my old stomping grounds and the neighbors who regaled my family with paella and much else over thirty years ago. I was only in the area for three days, but that was enough time for another round of paella and a full night of village gossip. Much had changed and much hadn't. Vineyards now stood beneath the ramparts of St. Paul and there was no red fox that I could see. The shepherd was gone. He had died hideously after having been struck by lightning while tending his flock on the hillside framed by my neighbors' window. I thought of Alphonse Daudet and his story of a mountain shepherd who lived close to the stars, a story that now felt uncomfortably real. I looked down at the house where I had helped raise two children and written a novel about an expat from Oklahoma who lived in France.

"*Dis donc, Linda. Tu parles bien maintenant. Comment t'as fait ces progrès en français?*"

I overcame my astonishment long enough to thank our old neighbor and mumbled something about having good teachers.

I didn't tell him about the things I couldn't do and changed the subject.

How about that ideal course I dreamed of in an earlier chapter? Details have changed, though it's as eclectic as ever. The *dictée* business with Pivot never happened, but one day when I'm feeling spunky I've got a DIY replica on my bookshelf. Purchased years ago in Paris and called *La dictée pour les nuls*, it comes with text, a CD of the *dictée* itself, and an inviting foreword written by Anna Gavalda, an author Claire introduced us to at The Carlyle. My book group at Alliance continues and I do another kind of workout on a stationary bike at the gym while watching and listening to something on the Internet, be that *Les carnets de Julie*, *La grande librairie*, or whatever delights me at the moment. Sometimes it's OK to be fickle and that's where I agree with this particular definition of the heart of the artichoke. I've known many loves thanks to the French language and culture. Today it's the insanely rich content on the Internet. Tomorrow, who knows? A recent exhibit of medieval bestiaries at the Getty Center, many of which were translated into French, was pretty stunning, so maybe I'll dive into a thirteenth-century manuscript about mythical animals next. I'm kidding, of course, but that some loves will fade and others appear to hold learners in their thrall — and keep them learning something in the process — is part of the promise I would hold out to anyone willing to taste an artichoke and take a trip, with or without a suitcase.

C   Earlier this month, *La grande librairie* celebrated Daniel Pennac. Crossing paths with him again as this book comes to a close hardly seems like a coincidence. Interviewed about *La loi du rêveur*, his most recent fiction, Pennac recalled his life as a teacher when teens who had "broken up with writing" were entrusted to him and when a dream brought on healing — the dream he had about them one night and shared in class the next day. So eager were they to share theirs in return that *la cueillette des rêves* became a ritual, for dreams must be "harvested" — i.e., noted — to be remembered. The notes were discussed but never shown. Not until Pennac offered to transcribe them himself did these kids, sentenced to a lifetime of failure by his predecessors, dare expose their writing again. And so began another ritual: *la dictée des rêves*. Dictated to Pennac, who lay them on the board "dressed in Sunday clothes," impeccably spelled and punctuated, the good-looking dreams did wonders. They restored confidence and sparked the desire to learn: the path to writing, and writing well, had been found.

How long and uneven it was Pennac didn't say. Nor did he say how he walked *ses rêveurs* to the place with the view, all the way to where the path ends, or forks into smaller ones. The harvest of dreams celebrates intuition but leaves another of his talents untold: the ability to sustain interest in learning — possibly the most important of teaching skills, and one Linda has developed for herself. With surprise twists and turns and mystery destinations, piecemeal learning offers the perfectionist little to hold on to but yields "larger wholes" that propel *l'aventurière* forward. And far she will go, for the adventurer has become a fluent learner.

As have I — by writing this book. By far the steepest, longest, and bumpiest path I've had to walk, yet an experience I embraced wholeheartedly.

How did that happen? I'd be lying if I said I devised or even followed a plan. Writing and I met the way friends do — because we're a good match. I am creative, reflective, and slow; curious about words and the ties that bind them; I delight in quiet, alone time; and love building stuff. Whether Linda had all this figured out or not, her invitation to coauthor a book was spot-on.

That it came with behind-the-scenes sweat and mess, countless weekends of it, was the challenge I had yet to face. That I did is something of a miracle. The roots of motivation are too deep to dig out, but I will attest to the word's origin, "to move," for I was set in motion.

It all started with music, the music of my own words long choked by the idea that more was better, until one day I was able to hear it — even tell whether it was good or not. Oh. So *juste* in *le mot juste* describes music as much as it does norms or precision. And — more news — *chanter juste* doesn't require a native tongue. What it takes is rehearsing, which, extraordinarily, has reignited my curiosity about a language I speak and write fluently. My interest to further explore it has been spiraling upward since I realized my words could sing, and sing in tune.

I must here take a detour to the first — and eerily prescient? — poem I wrote in English, long before this book:

Layers of time

A pile of them

How many

How high

Until noise becomes

Music again

It celebrates rebirth but echoes the very process that has unfolded since I began hearing words, layers upon layers of them in the pursuit of music.

With it came another shift — one promised by Fred Vargas. "*L'effet curieux de la langue qui se met à bouger toute seule*" is not only curious: to feel the pull of language is thrilling. The more I write, the more English "moves by itself" — and the more I follow in its wake. Now and again, I'll notice a shape in the distance, catch a melody and the rustling of rhythms until all blends together and a word stands out, no longer foreign. I cherish these moments — when thesaurus and Google surrender their stronghold, when language emerges from beneath the surface.

Summer, unusually hot and dry in Alsace one year, caused a water shortage for the neighbors living up the hill from our house. I accompanied one of them in his search for a mountain spring. He found it right where the butt end of the forked stick he was holding with both hands pointed. "We mustn't scare her away," he said, delicately excavating the soil from the area, "for she might flee to pursue her course hidden and undisturbed." There are obvious parallels between water and motivation — both flow, empower, sometimes dry out — but never had I thought of them as having minds of their own. As water percolated through rocks and dirt, I understood it was teaching me a lesson. Tread lightly.

Apprendre à apprendre. There lies our heart. ❧

Acknowledgments

It's impossible to adequately thank our pseudonymous friends at The Carlyle for a book group that animated our lives and our Saturday afternoons for years. We've altered their names, but not their love of French language and culture.

We remain grateful to The Carlyle for letting us linger. It was the perfect home for our quirky literary escapades.

Nadine Juton's elegant book club presentations and deep readings of classic and contemporary literature at the Alliance Française de Los Angeles were a joy. *Un grand merci pour toutes ces belles années.*

This has been a family affair in so many ways. My sister-in-law and our graphic designer, Margot Asahina, came up with just the right imagery for our dialogue. Her artistry appears on every page.

The attention to detail of our copy editor, Califia Suntree, is beyond extraordinary. We have been both inspired and energized by her range of knowledge in French and English.

A very special thanks to Michael Dambrosia, photographer and magician *sans pareil.*

Where would any of us be without a network of supportive friends? Jill Marinoff, to whom I am forever thankful for our long-standing friendship and her impeccable comic timing in another language. Cherished pals Catherine Dunne, Kate Hinkle, Dolly Rosen, and Susan

Dalton, inveterate travelers all, lent great energy to this enterprise. Linda Upton, whose generosity of spirit will never be forgotten. It may be that Marlette Betesh understood the nature of this project before I did. When the going got rough, another fine Susan Chehak short story appeared, reminding me to trust the process. I am deeply indebted to Teresa Miller, who writes and befriends with equal grace. Insights from Colleen Craig, writer, editor, and narrative strategist, have been invaluable over the years. Novelist Aimee Liu sparked fresh conversations about French language and literature. Jo Giese and Diane Leslie, two very gifted writers, have known exactly when and how to ask about a work so long in progress. Their belief that this project would one day come to fruition helped more than they know. Fellow Francophile Carol Perry, ever "ready for the new" and a glass of red wine at 92 years of age, has filled me with faith in this enterprise and so much more.

Merci aux amis à Saint-Paul de Vence. Les souvenirs tiennent toujours.

My brother Randolph has been a tremendous support and cheerleader throughout.

Deepest thanks go to my children, Savannah and Christopher, and their father, Mamdouh, for allowing me to share their stories as well as my own.

Without the continuous encouragement and input from my husband, Bob Asahina, this project would never have gotten off the ground. His contribution is immeasurable, as ever. To say I lucked out when I met him is woefully inadequate.

And to Claire, patient friend and tireless coauthor. We did it!

— *Linda Phillips Ashour*

My love goes to my family — the tender heart of it.

To my mother and father, exceptional in their own ways, who contributed to this work more than they know. *Je leur dois le goût du beau et de l'effort.*

To Anne, Louis, and Jacques, loving sister and brothers, for what flows between us.

To my nieces and nephews, Lise, Laure, Louis, and Paul, whose resolve helped forge my own. Tata Z loves you.

Tuulikki and Perry Wolff would be proud of me. They were parents, mentors, and friends. I treasure the memories.

Marie-Anne Klein, *tendre marraine* and first-grade teacher, kindled my love of reading and writing. The story of Fleur-de-Lupin has retained the magic of first times.

Dr. P, who, and where, would I be without you? You have taught me the language of the self. Becoming fluent has changed my life.

I have honed my teaching skills thanks to my UN colleagues and friends, and to the many ideas and accomplishments that brought us closer over the years. *L'aventure continue.*

I am grateful to Adrian Hills, French-speaking section chief of the Capacity Development and Operational Training Service, for his support and the example he sets for the organization.

Artichoke hearts of various shapes and forms grace the walls of my Brooklyn apartment. My admiration and thanks go to the wonderful *artistes peintres* who've captured them: Anne Lerognon, Cristina Pérez-Cordón, and Huguette Martel.

I could not be more pleased with my author photo. Céline Charpigny made me feel beautiful, happy, and free that summer evening in our mountains. *Merci l'artiste!*

To the dear and close friends who never stopped asking about the book, I say thank you. Your words of encouragement were just what I needed.

We are deeply indebted to the TBR Books publishing team, and to Fabrice Jaumont in particular for his immediate enthusiasm for, and faith in, our artichoke. The book's second draft was so worth the hard work.

And to Linda and Bob, precious teammates. What you saw in me has materialized in ways I could not have imagined. For this, I am forever grateful.

— Claire Lerognon

About the Authors

Linda Phillips Ashour is the author of four novels: *Speaking in Tongues, Joy Baby, Sweet Remedy*, and *A Comforting Lie. Speaking in Tongues* is the story of an expat from Oklahoma that was written when she lived in the South of France. Her articles and book reviews have appeared in the *New York Times Book Review*, the *New York Sun, Mia*, and the *Weekly Standard*. She has published short fiction in the *Paris Review* and the *North American Review* and was a contributor to *My Father Married Your Mother: Dispatches from the Blended Family*. She has taught writing at UCLA Extension, received a Beck fellowship from Denison University, and been a fellow at Yaddo. She lives in Los Angeles with her husband.

Claire Lerognon is a language and communications specialist at the United Nations headquarters in New York City. Her interest in languages and language acquisition led to a colorful career teaching French to students ranging from preschoolers to diplomats and the UN's global staff. She is currently part of the Language and Communications Training Unit where she specializes in training design and development geared towards fostering multilingualism in the organization. *The Heart of an Artichoke* is her first book — and boldest learning venture yet. Claire lives in Brooklyn, New York.

About TBR Books

TBR Books is a program of the Center for the Advancement of Languages, Education, and Communities. We publish researchers and practitioners who seek to engage diverse communities on topics related to education, languages, cultural history, and social initiatives. We translate our books in a variety of languages to further expand our impact.

Our Books in English

One Good Question by Rhonda Broussard

Can We Agree to Disagree? by Agathe Laurent and Sabine Landolt

Immigrant Dreams: A Memoir by Barbara Goldowsky

Salsa Dancing in Gym Shoes by Tammy Oberg de la Garza and Alyson Leah Lavigne

The Clarks of Willsborough Point by Darcey Hale

Beyond Gibraltar by Maristella de Panniza Lorch

The Gift of Languages by Fabrice Jaumont and Kathleen Stein-Smith

Two Centuries of French Education by Jane Ross

The Bilingual Revolution by Fabrice Jaumont

Our Books in Other Languages

Le projet Colibri by Vickie Frémont

Peshtigo 1871 by Charles Mercier

Conversations sur le bilinguisme by Fabrice Jaumont

Sénégalais de l'étranger by Maya Angela Smith

Our Children's Books

Rose Alone by Sheila Flynn DeCosse

Rainbows, Masks, and Ice Cream by Deana Sobel Lederman

Marimba by Christine Hélot and Patricia Velasco

The Blue Dress by Teboho Moja

Immunity Fun by Dounia Stewart-McMeel

Math for All by Mark Hansen

Would you Help me Choose a Pet? by Gail Foster

Super Korean New Years with Grandma by Mary Chi-Whi Kim and Eunjoo Feaster

Our books are available on our website and on all major online bookstores as paperback and e-book. Some of our books have been translated into Arabic, Chinese, English, French, German, Italian, Japanese, Polish, Russian, Spanish. For a listing of all books published by TBR Books, information on our series, or for our submission guidelines for authors, visit our website.

www.tbr-books.org

About CALEC

The Center for the Advancement of Languages, Education, and Communities is a nonprofit organization focused on promoting multilingualism, empowering multilingual families, and fostering cross-cultural understanding. The Center's mission is in alignment with the United Nations' Sustainable Development Goals. Our mission is to establish language as a critical life skill, through developing and implementing bilingual education programs, promoting diversity, reducing inequality, and helping to provide quality education. Our programs seek to protect world cultural heritage and support teachers, authors, and families by providing the knowledge and resources to create vibrant multilingual communities.

We have served multiple communities through our flagship programs, which include:

- TBR Books, our publishing arm, which publishes research, essays, and case studies with a focus on innovative ideas for education, languages, and cultural development;

- Our online platform that provides information, coaching, and support to multilingual families seeking to create dual-language programs in schools;

- NewYorkinFrench.net, an online platform which provides collaborative tools to support the Francophone community and the diversity of people who speak French.

We also support parents and educators interested in advancing languages, education, and communities. For more information and ways you can support our mission, visit our website.

www.calec.org